Ragbag to Riches

JOHN THOMSON

ISBN: **1533344272**
ISBN-13: **978-1533344274**

DEDICATION

This book is dedicated to Darrell Clarke and his back to back promotion winning squad which made club history on the 7th May 2016.

The following pages are also dedicated to Helen, Beth, Meg, Jake and the rest of my family. Love you to the stars and back! UTG

ACKNOWLEDGMENTS

Massive thanks to Andy Colley for designing the book cover. We got there in the end mate! Many thanks also to the Gasheads who gave me their permission to use their photographs from 7th May 2016. UTG

PROLOGUE

And in the beginning there was nothing. And from this eternal nothingness was born a light. And her name was Avon.

In timeless being she gazed alone into the darkness around her and then cried out for love to hold. And her wish was granted by the Gods who ruled over the emptiness of nothingness.

Avon held them close. A boy and a girl whom she loved equally with full of heart. But unbeknown to Avon - the Gods of nothingness had sowed the seed of balance within the essence of their new creations.

A boy and a girl. Ted and Irene.

Irene was gentle and kind and her strength was of heart. Beautiful to behold - her wisdom and generosity and love of all would see all of the nothingness drawn to the very centre of her existence. And it was commonplace for the Gods of emptiness to gaze down on her as all of the small, furry and cute animals which dwelled within the vastness of nothingness danced around her and cuddled her as the birds perched on her outstretched arms as she danced and sang in joy.

Ted sat in a dark corner - dribbling and demented.

And thus it came to be that balance was born.

1. TWILIGHT

There's something about the twilight of day that I love.

Not quite a beginning. Not quite an end. But somewhere in between where both embrace and something magical can be seen and felt.

Of golden light which offers a stillness in time - a stillness in time which can etch forever memories to hold close to heart until that day comes. And who knows - maybe it's those pictures from past which are offered at that time to quieten the transition from here to there?

But whatever the truth may be - I know in my own heart that one of my own twilight memories will be the one from the gold of light which followed a right foot tap-in and what was to follow was a beautiful bedlam. And to be honest - I'm not sure I'll ever experience such an incredible experience ever again.

I say that purely from the events which preceded the right foot and they took place over a very short period of time - within the infinite measure of time. Two years is nothing to hold a time of everything. And it's as if everything good and right has happened in the nine months which have just passed and it's as if the twilight of our own time has arrived for us - the twilight end from day which began a long time ago and now holds close a dawn of gold from which the light of many stars now shine down on our own time.

Stars like Clarke, Lockyer, Taylor, Lines, Leadbitter, Bodin, Harrison, Gaffney and so many others.

Brown. The beautiful bedlam which ensued from his right foot transcended anything I've ever experienced upon the steps of the Blackthorn End. It was as if our traditions and passion - locked within every heart who witnessed his goal - exploded forth with an energy which probably stopped time as eleven thousand voices announced our arrival to a time which is our time. It was an energy which erupted with elation and relief following a relegation; to the fight back and then to another promotion. And so club history was made.

For me - that experience was to meander from that special place and wander and weave into the seconds and minutes and hours which followed. It was an experience which was to wind its way through time and into the golden light which fell upon Gloucester Road not long after the final whistle blew - to a moment like no other which saw our new owner being held aloft on the shoulders of the blue and white faithful amid the jubilation in song which cried to the golden light, "We've got our Rovers back!"

Gloucester Road, 7th May 2016

So when I say I'm not sure I'll ever experience that experience again - I'm not sure I ever will. But then again - I don't have to because I was there and I saw it and I heard it and I felt it. And I'm truly grateful to have been part of it all. And I wasn't alone in that experience.

Over eleven thousand of you were there with me too and I know there were thousands of other Gasheads from far and wide who were listening to the radio and monitoring the internet for live commentary and the latest updates on various sports websites.

We were in it together and we were watching and listening from different locations all over the world. And I just happened to be one of so many who were fortunate enough to be at the Memorial Stadium on the 7th of May 2016.

I'll never forget it and I will always consider myself extremely fortunate to have witnessed what many now describe as one of the most important days in the history of Bristol Rovers. And what I hope to do in the pages which follow is to do the best I can to deliver the story of how that day came to be from my own perspective as a supporter following the release of my first book, *'Faithful and True - A Gashead's Story'* in December 2015.

What follows now is what was to take place after the release of that book - a book which tells the story of how I fell in love with this incredible football club after moving to Bristol in 2010 and how my new partner, Helen, introduced me to *The Gas* - an introduction which has completely changed my life.

That book highlights our fightback from relegation to the Football Conference to our return to the Football League following a dramatic play off final at Wembley in May last year. And it also covers the first half of our 2015/2016 League Two campaign.

I'll do my very best to avail from going over 'old ground'. But some topics are bound to re-emerge and these include a certain team from Nailsworth which has left me concerned that cannibalism is alive and well in English football; the infamous Memorial Stadium chicken tikka pie;

the lost civilisation of Yeovil Town and the continued success of one of our favourite sons - Nathan Blissett.

As mentioned in the first publication - I'm originally from Glasgow. So I can't promise no sweary words. It's a bit like asking a Ted to not dribble. But I'll do my very best and I can absolutely guarantee that I'll do whatever is humanly possible to avoid using the 'C' word. But please understand - the rivalry between two sides in Bristol is intense and so there will be occasions when you'll see 'City' on your page. So I'll apologise for that right now.

So let's get into this story about how we won automatic promotion to League One a few weeks ago. And to be honest - I still can't believe we did it. It's still too beautifully unreal to be real and I think a lot of that has to do with what I experienced on the steps of the Blackthorn End just after Browner tapped in that goal. I've never known or felt or seen such elation before. Don't get me wrong - I've been around and I've seen things and done things during my time. But nothing like that. That was and I'm sure will always remain unique in my experience of life.

Since beginning to follow The Gas in 2013 - I've been fortunate enough to be part of many a joyous celebration with the rest of my blue and white family on the steps of the North Terrace and on the road at grounds across England. But what was to follow just before the twilight of day - on that day - is unlikely to be equalled.

So how did we do it?

Well, my answer to that question doesn't take much thought. We did it together. We all did it together after finding unity following relegation and it's a togetherness which remains with all of us. Owner. Chairman. Manager. Squad. Staff. Supporters. Everyone.

But you really don't need me to tell you that. You already know that. And you know that because of one unique thing. You know that because this isn't just my story - it's your story too. You were there and we all witnessed it together. And what we witnessed on that day which ended in the twilight of sun was nothing less than a once in a lifetime experience.

I don't really remember much about our winning goal to be honest. I know I was there and I know I saw what happened. But it's difficult to explain.

Blackthorn End, 7th May 2016

It's as if my eyes were working - but not much else. I suppose my brain must have been switched on because hindsight has blessed me with the recollections of what happened during those final moments. But the grey matter was simply storing the slow motion images of a sea of frenzied blue and white noise which seemed to be doing its best to do three things at the same time.

Now, hindsight has rammed my head with a visual trinity of massed attempts just after a left footed defender did something with his right foot. And that's a bit impressive in my books. Not because a left footed player did something with his right foot. It's probably more to do with the fact that I don't have a right foot and I've become a bit fascinated by that particular part of the human anatomy.

Don't get me wrong. I'm not some kind of deviant who now has a thing for feet. That would be completely untrue. I'm a deviant who has a thing for lots of things and feet are just one of many on my list of 'things' which grab my attention and would have probably seen me do a certain amount of time in a Victorian asylum. And in some strange way - I think I might have enjoyed that.

But I'm digressing. You'll find I do that. I'll try my best not to. But I do struggle sometimes to write in a linear way. It's just not the way my head works. One moment I'm telling the whole world I have a 'things' list - then I find a few minutes have passed because I'm dwelling on what Ollie has just said after the Accrington Wimbledon Play-Off Semi-Final about Akinfenwa eating his twin brother.

It's madness. No, not the madness in my head - the madness that once again I find myself deeply concerned that cannibalism is the new 'thing' with certain football clubs.

Forest Green Rovers. If you've read *Faithful and True* - you'll be aware of my analysis of the Nailsworth side following our encounter with them towards the end of our Bananarama campaign.

As we all know - it was hardly a cruel summer for us. But Ollie's comment about a player devouring a loved one has once again sparked that fear I had when I was writing my first book about falling in love with the mighty *Gas*. And that particular horror concerning munching on folk was courtesy of witnessing our lads having to endure ninety minutes against a side which looked more akin to gnawing on ball boys as opposed to broccoli.

I'm genuinely not writing this to get a cheap laugh at the expense of the unfortunate appearance of FGR players. Seriously - have you seen them? Were you there on that sunny April evening last year and did you see them emerge out of the tunnel alongside our lads? Fuck me - talk about beauty and the beast? And the beast looked hungry! But not as hungry-looking as Akinfenwa. I reckon the whole Womble clan would just be a satisfactory starter for him. Actually - come to think of it – the Common's been looking a bit littered lately!

But these are the opening pages of a book which will focus on the triumphant season we've just experienced and I'd rather not dwell too much on eating loved ones and what happened last season. So many pages remain and I'm sure I'll drop into the New Lawn again at some point within the paragraphs which await your pleasure - or displeasure for those of a sensitive nature.

For those of you who've read *Faithful and True, A Gashead's Story* - you'll be fully aware of what's coming for you and you'll already have what you need to help you through it. For those who haven't read the first book – it's probably best to stop reading now and go and get yourself some valium, some vodka and some chloroform. And no - you don't need all of that to help you cope with the pages which follow. I just find they're handy to have because they offer an excellent night in if you're on your own and you've got nothing to do.

But please try and stay with me. There will be times when you may feel empty, lost and confused and not quite sure why you're committing precious minutes of your life by observing what's in front of your eyes. But the least said about a certain 'bench with subs which is made in Bristol' - the better! Harsh? Maybe. But I do have a serious resentment with them. Every time I watch them present the programme - I'm immediately hurled back in time to when I was a young child and all I can see is Gonzo. No! Not that kind of Gonzo! I wasn't watching hardcore porn at the age of ten! That happened the following year! I'm referring to Gonzo from *The Muppets*. He always made me feel really uncomfortable. Huge, hanging nose. Wide-eyed stare. Wicked Witch of the West voice. I used to have to hide behind the sofa when he appeared. And when I knew he'd gone - I'd take a peek at the screen and I'd usually see Statler and Waldorf. Now you get it!

So where was I? Oh yeah, Lee Brown's right foot on the 7th of May - just two weeks ago.

Now as I've already mentioned - it was all it bit bizarre when it happened and it genuinely felt for me as if time had stood still and everything seemed to be moving in slow motion. And I'm not just referring to the moment the winner hit the back of the net. I'm talking about the minutes which actually preceded the tap in.

Everything felt slow and heavy. It genuinely felt as if time had slowed down and when Taylor missed that 'sitter' towards the end of the regulation ninety - it felt as if time had actually stopped.

But the strange thing was - even though it felt as if time itself had abandoned the Memorial Stadium - it also felt as if whatever time had left behind was racing ahead at high speed.

Now, I'm no Stephen Hawking - but I'm absolutely convinced that some kind of time and space ripple was smashed open after Matty's shot went wide of the right hand post and I'm pretty sure Hawking would have been very interested in the theory of everything that was happening just off Filton Avenue at around 4.45pm on the seventh day of May.

The hunch was pretty much universally felt that something extraordinary was going to happen and this feeling was sensed by many among the blue and white faithful before the game. But the hunch was deliberately hushed down. I actually know of someone who quietly and confidently predicted the accurate outcome of the match just an hour before the game kicked-off. And that incident will be discussed in a later chapter which will also include other 'predictions' regarding Bristol Rovers match outcomes.

But what I will say is we're now seriously considering opening a new business in our house and I'm also contemplating having a new front gate designed in the shape of a pentagon. And as for dancing around naked under the pale moonlight? Well, Mildenhall still owes us all one and if we decide to indulge in that kind of barefaced behaviour - then he's duly obliged to get the opening ceremony underway in our back garden!

To be honest - I actually felt naked just before Browner used his right foot. I felt lost and empty and alone. I didn't know where to look after the Taylor miss and the fact that there was a giant head standing right in front of me in the Blackthorn End didn't help much either.

When I say giant head - I don't mean a head on its own. That would be a bit weird - even for me. I mean there was an actual person standing right in front of me and his head was massive. And I remember thinking at the time - he's either holding his breath with all the stress and it's causing his head to inflate - or he was born that way and I can only imagine how very unpopular he was with his mum after he arrived. And I'm sure his dad wasn't best pleased either - but for a completely different reason!

So the massive hole in time and space before the second goal felt like some kind of vortex had descended on and whirled around the Mem as the white clouds above cast a grey blanket of light down and upon eleven thousand uneasy souls. It fell upon our hope of something extraordinary happening and seemed to smother us in a moment in time which time had abandoned. And yet it also seemed as if we were still hurtling towards something - because even though time was no longer with us - there remained the sense that this was our time and the Gods of Football had already decided on that outcome. And then it happened.

The Gods of Football guided the ball to Jake Gosling and Jermaine Easter. It was a genius move.

The deities knew that Browner needed time to get up into the eighteen yard box to tap the ball in from a rebound off the post. And the only player who could hit the post from inside the eighteen yard box - was Taylor.

But Matty had to get the ball before he could get an accurate strike onto the right hand side upright - so that the left footed defender could tap it in with his right. And that's why the supreme beings chose Gosling and Easter.

They knew they could count on them pushing and passing their way through the Daggers defence so that Taylor was gifted the ball. And it worked. Matty had all the time in the world to twist and turn and take aim. And then he let loose at the perfect moment in time in his space - because Lee was now also inside the eighteen yard box and heading for the left hand post.

Taylor struck the ball with a precision like no other. The strike was sublime and the angle of the rebound fell beautifully to Browner's right foot for him to tap it down and in.

History is synonymous with time. It refers to an event in a place at a time. And when Lee Brown scored that goal - history was made. Maybe that's why the vortex from above descended on the Memorial Stadium and it was felt and sensed in the moments just before that tap-in hit the back of the net? Maybe what we felt was the imminent arrival of history being made? And maybe the Gods of Football decided that for history to be made just off Filton Avenue -

the goal had to be scored with only two minutes of injury time remaining. And why? Well, maybe it was the perfect time? Maybe the only time - considering what was happening elsewhere? Our time of right foot didn't give Accrington a lot of time to score against Stevenage. So it just had to be that way to ensure history was made at the Memorial Stadium.

So much more of what happened on that incredible day is still to come - but not yet. That will be shared later – including the three things which I saw thousands of Gasheads doing just after Lee Brown scored the winner. Here's a clue to the first one. They were trying to escape from the Blackthorn End. I know, I know - that doesn't make sense. But trust me - it will later on when you read it.

But it wasn't just about that one day for me. Yes it was incredible – but what made it so were the matches and results and events off the pitch which brought together a fervour which may just be a first for our club. I'm by no way dismissing successes and glories of times gone by - I'm simply saying that so much was to happen between December and May which contributed towards a stunning end to our 2015/2016 season.

It was an end like no other - literally - since our time began in 1883. And I'm going to do the best I can to share what I experienced with you - because it was a privilege to be part of it all.

The final paragraphs within *Faithful and True* ended with the story in early December last year. What comes now is what was to follow...

2 FORTRESS

There's a place that's now very special to me and I've only visited it once. It's fondly referred to as the *Fortress* by Rovers supporters and the nickname itself defines the very heart and fight which our club is proud to hold dear.

Twerton Park - the Bath City ground - was our shared home for ten years when we had nowhere else to go after leaving our spiritual home at Eastville in 1986. And my understanding is that the departure was the result of fire damage to the stadium amid financial problems - so Bristol Rovers were left homeless and the Bath club took us in and allowed us to share their ground.

It was known as our *Fortress* for good reason. Bristol Rovers were pretty much unbeatable during this time at this place in our club's history and 2-1 victories after being 1-0 down were commonplace. And so the nickname was born.

So many fond memories of those times were shared to me during my early days as a Gashead by other supporters who'd become part of my life - with the most memorable being the 3-0 victory against rivals City on the 2nd of May 1990.

The more I heard about the Twerton years - the more I wanted to know. And so - with only two final chapters to write for *Faithful and True* at the beginning of December last year - I just woke up one morning and drove to the Bath City ground to script the final words for the book in the place where Bruno and Ollie netted the goals which will forever be etched in the hearts and minds of Rovers supporters everywhere.

It was just a few days following Matty's hat trick against Wycombe Wanderers and it was a beautiful sunny winter's morning. And what was to happen to me at the ground took me completely by surprise.

Writing the final chapters whilst sitting just above the dugouts is something I'll never forget - because as I was writing - I was also receiving messages from other Rovers supporters and they were sharing with me their own personal memories of watching the blue and white quarters play at the *Fortress*.

The number of messages was a bit overwhelming and I felt humbled for two reasons. The first was that people were sharing their own memories with me as I sat in the very place they were referring to. And it really did feel as if all of the passion and love of our club from those times could still be felt. It was strange as I sat and took it all in. Me - a man who had never watched *The Gas* play at the ground –

Twerton, December 2015

yet I felt immensely proud to be there. And the second reason was I was simply there. I was there and I could just sit and look at the pitch and see the goals being scored in a replay in my mind from the video footage I'd seen and just sit and almost feel what I imagined it felt like back in 1990.

I really hope this doesn't sound weird - but it really did feel as if I could sense those days and the thousands of you who were there during those times. I'll never forget it. And when I'd finished writing - I just didn't want to leave. So I just sat by myself and enjoyed being there.

It was a wee bit special for me and I really don't care if I sound like a sentimental, soppy sod. I really don't care because I can be a sentimental, soppy sod.

After a while, I offered my thanks to the ground staff who allowed me the time to sit and write and I returned to my car. And that's where and when it happened.

I just sat and became really emotional. And I don't mind saying that. I started to get a bit teary because the thought of my club being homeless actually hurt me. We'd only recently achieved something to be really proud of after fighting our way out of non-league football and back into the Football League - a league in which we were holding our own and were actually sitting 10th in the table as I sat in my car. So to think that we were once without a home and could have easily disappeared altogether had an effect on me. And I knew why…

There was a deep and profound personal resonance and it hit me hard. You see - I know what it feels like to have nowhere to go and to have no home. I know what it feels like to not be wanted and to drift amid bad times. I would never want that for or allow that to happen to someone or something I love.

Words cannot really describe what it feels like. And for that reason - I simply fell in love with Twerton. They gave us a home when we had no home and - even though I wasn't living in Bristol during our time there - I will always be grateful to Bath City FC for sharing their ground with us and I'm really looking forward to our pre-season friendly at the ground in a few weeks.

I may or may not share more about what happened to me during that time in my life later in this book. I'm not sure yet. I did write a little bit about it in *Faithful and True* and I touched on it only to highlight how I ended up in Bristol. But there was a lot more behind the reason why I ended up in this part of the country. So we'll see. If it sits appropriately at some point in the pages which follow - then I'll write about it.

At the end of the day - I'm a writer. I have to write the truth - even if it makes me feel a bit uneasy. And to be honest - I do feel that my past played a massive part in the reason why I fell in love with the club. Just thinking about it now as I write these words – it's probably what happened to me in my past which pushed me towards committing to follow Bristol Rovers the day we were sent down in 2014.

I know what it feels like to be relegated as a person. So I decided to join Helen and our other Gashead friends in supporting Darrell and his squad at as many games as possible. And it was during this time that I fell in love with our club.

Later - I once heard a Gashead say, "We've always had nothing but we've always given everything!" And that comment confirmed the truth as to why I became drawn to the supporters of Irene. People filled with fight and heart no matter the odds and that's an incredible potential to be proud of. And it was only a few months ago that that potential was to be acknowledged and invested in!

So I probably will write more about that part of my life because I'm convinced that experience played a deeply personal part in me deciding to follow the Rovers.

I'm generally fearless regarding anything else which I write about - even if it means attracting the wrath of the cannibals of Nailsworth or the 'people' from Yeovil whom time forgot or the followers of the Dark Lord who we know as 'them down the road'. But I'd like to think they all know that my criticisms come from a caring place and that the bombardments in prose are designed to help them to take a long hard look in the mirror. And if they can see through the bloodshot eyes and demented gumsy grins - they'll see that much help is needed. And if their acceptance of that is embraced - then my job here is done! Although - to be honest - I have a funny feeling it'll take more than two books for that to happen. So I'll soldier on and write as many as I can over the years to come.

But they are and always will be incidental to anything I write. My passion for scripting is now devoted to the blue and white in a way which I enjoy. I loved writing the first book and I'm loving writing this one too. And I think I always will write about our club because what I see and hear at matches gives me great pleasure now in my life.

So it was on that sunny winter's day during the first week in December 2015 that I drove away from Twerton Park. And as I headed back to Hanham - I knew that something unique had just happened to me. I'd been following Bristol Rovers in the present since 2013. Now - driving away from the Bath City ground - I knew I'd made a very real and tangible connection with the club's past. And that left me filled with pride.

I'm proud to be a Gashead. I always will be. I'll stand by our gaffer and his squad and the rest of you without question. And I'll always look ahead with optimism regarding what the future holds for all of us. But I couldn't have imagined what lay ahead for me and thousands of other supporters in the weeks and months that were to follow my departure from *The Fortress*. I don't think anyone could've predicted that…

3 GINGERS AND EXORCISMS

It took the arrival of a certain Irish striker from Cambridge United for me to admit I was ginger.

For forty eight years - I'd been uttering utterances which were utterly treasonous to my own species.

For almost half a century - when the 'G' word was put to me - my reply was either, "No. It just goes dark when it's long. If I get it cut - you'll see I'm a dirty blonde kind of colour!" OR "No. I'm not ginger. I'm Scandinavian blonde. My grandfather was from Norway!"

Now, the latter is very true. My dad's dad was in fact a direct descendent of the Vikings and I know the Nordic gene is in my blood because I love the sea and I love being on boats and I get a weird feeling when I'm in IKEA and I love their meatballs.

So it's a no brainer that I've got Norse blood in me. I've also been known to indulge in a wee bit of pillaging in my time. But to be honest - that word has an entirely different meaning in Glasgow and has more to do with 'spreading the love' as opposed to travelling far from home with the intent of bashing and robbing locals. Although, to be fair, that kind of behaviour can still be found in certain parts north of the border. No. Not north of Hadrian's Wall. North of the Bishopsworth border in a place called Ashton Gate.

I had to drive past that place a few weeks ago. I was on my way to the airport to pick up a mate from Scotland who was spending a few days in Bristol on business. And to be honest (I'm being serious now) when I was hurling past the home of 'them down the road' - I felt something awful.

It was as if some kind of heaviness - some kind of 'darkness unseen' - was smothering all that will never be good from within and around the ground and it made me feel terribly uneasy. And I'm not joking.!

The sense of foreboding was so awful that I actually felt drawn to pull over to stop and look and try to find the source of the emptiness which I felt was seeping out from somewhere?

It was hellish - yet it seemed to be pulling me in to look closer to find the ghastly truth which resides deep within the bowels of what lays beneath this awful place. But I was lucky. I always wear my seven pointed star around my neck and I'm convinced it intervened in cutting me free from being dragged into some kind of abyss.

But it did get me thinking. So I did a bit of digging. No, I didn't stop the car and start removing topsoil near that place. I'd only do that if my intention was to amass a skull collection - courtesy of ancient and contemporary human sacrifices which I'm sure do take place in that part of town.

No, I meant research into finding some answers as to why it feels so bad where 'them down the road' live. And my findings are startling! I hope you're ready for this?

My digging began with the meaning of 'Ashton'. It means 'Ash Tree Town'. Ash Tree? And with that - my twenty second research uncovered the shocking truth!

Ash trees are hugely symbolic within occult circles. They symbolise the connection between this world and the netherworld. And when I unveiled this hidden knowledge - that's when my Eureka moment hit me!

Ashton - the town connected to the underworld. Add a 'Gate' to the end and what do you get? Exactly! The Gateway to Hell!

So my new findings left me with an immense dilemma. I was torn between two ways of thinking.

Cerebral process number one informed me that 'them down the road' aren't responsible for the way they are and that the way they are is courtesy of them residing over the House of Hades. So could it be that they aren't their fault?

So with me being a sometimes benevolent soul (sometimes) I took some time out to ponder the possibility of 'cleansing' the area using pagan methods.

So my digging got deeper. But I was careful not to dig too deep and find hell myself. And it was at this time that I discovered 'smudging'!

Now, smudging is an old practice which involves burning sage in an area believed to be possessed by evil spirits. They used to do it during medieval times when the plague was rampant and people blamed the afflictions on the work of unholy entities. The symptoms were horrific. Folk could be found stumbling around, covered in seeping boils and foaming at the mouth whilst uttering incoherently as they shouted at the sky. Not entirely unlike what can be witnessed in and around Bedminster on a match day.

So my idea was a simple one. I get some sage and head down to where 'them down the road' live and begin wandering around with a ceramic bowl filled with the smouldering herb. It seemed to make sense to me and so I headed down to Asda to get what was needed.

Two pounds! That's how much a small jar of sage costs. Two quid!

So before I headed back to our house to see if there was any growing behind the shed - I looked at the Asda own brand and it only cost ninety five pence. But that just didn't feel right. If I was going to clear hell from Ashton Gate - I'd need the good stuff. But two pounds plus five pence for the plastic bag? I pondered the pros and cons for about one second and my verbal outcry from within was a typical response from a typical Glaswegian, "Fuck that!"

And with that 'fuck' I proceeded onto option two.

I did my best and my best took two weeks of intense online research and phone calls to clergy all over the land. But to no avail. I even tried some of my former journalist colleagues at Scottish Television - but it just wasn't to be. And in the end I just had to surrender to the fact that the Pope doesn't have a mobile phone because no one has his number.

So, the Supreme Pontiff's unwillingness to wander into Carphone Warehouse is the reason 'them down the road' will remain held by darkness - because my second plan was to have Ashton Gate and all the souls within and around undergo a mass exorcism. But if I can't get hold of Frank - then frankly - it ain't going to happen.

So I'm afraid they'll just have to continue in their suffering and maybe it's some kind of divine penance which has befallen that part of Bristol and to which no mortal man may intervene. And the more I think about it – the longer their torment should last!

So I pulled in the reigns and submitted to the truth that Karma can't be stopped. It exists for a reason and who am I to question it?

All I can say on this matter is this - whatever 'them down the road' did in a previous life must have been bad. I mean - just how bad do you have to be in a prior existence to end up in the here and now with a manager who sounds like Jo Pasquale?

So from those destined for the burny fire to a man on fire in December. Rory Gaffney! The on loan arrival to Darrel Clarke's squad set our game alight during the five weeks he spent with us. And he arrived at just the right time.

Fair play to Matty Taylor though. He'd just started to find the back of the net again and his announcement to all that he meant business took place on the first evening of Yuletide. And what a way to kick off the festive season!

They say lightning never strikes twice in the same place. So, how beautifully apt it was for Wycombe Wanderers to find out that strikes like lightening can indeed hit three times in the same place in twelve minutes. Mr Silverware take a bow! And from that result onwards - we were to remain unbeaten at the Mem for the rest of the season!

Taylor's three goal demolition of Wycombe came at a time when we'd been struggling to find the back of the net at home and it was causing a lot of concern. Our away performances were on form and we seemed to be scoring for fun having won six out of our first ten matches on the road. And then it all just seemed to come right. It all seemed to happen at the same time and that time was the perfect time for the new face from the Abbey Stadium.

Matty was finding his confidence and his form and the introduction of the flame-haired Irishman from Cambridge a few weeks earlier offered the piece that was missing.

Tall. Strong. Fast. Gaffers slotted right in and his style of play in aggressively running the channels and holding up the ball was and remains a pleasure to watch. And he doesn't just chase the ball - he hurtles towards to ball as if he's chasing down something which lays beyond the ball after he receives what his outstretched hands request from another team mate. I just love watching him play and I know I'm not alone in that one. And I'm not just saying that because he's one of us - a ginger.

I know he's become a favourite for many a Gashead and his presence was felt almost immediately after Shaun Derry gave the nod for his on loan departure to our club. He may not have fitted in with Derry's plans - but it was another perfect move from Clarke. But was it too good?

It almost was too good because Gaffers ran riot wearing our blue and white quarters. It did take him a short amount of time to make his scoring prowess known after making his debut away to Exeter in late November and his first came away to Daggenham just seven days before Santa arrived.

That seemed to give him the scent of blood and he ended up running amok against Leyton Orient ten days later. His second goal in the second half of that match is one of my top three of the season. And it was most definitely my own personal football highlight during the season of goodwill.

It was a fairly quiet Christmas for us and I suppose in many ways - we did what everyone else was doing. We were indulging in a food orgy beneath a flashing tree.

We couldn't go to the Wimbledon away match because our actual Christmas celebration took place on Boxing Day - courtesy of family arrangements. But by all accounts - we didn't miss much and it sounded as if the space allocated to our fans was a bit of a shambles. So Helen and I couldn't wait to get out of the house and away from the TV on the 28th of December for the Leyton Orient match at the Mem.

Don't get me wrong - I do enjoy the festive season – but I start to go a bit stir crazy after Christmas Eve. That's my favourite night. That's the one I look forward to and I think it's because that's when the true magic of Christmas is felt.

It's more the anticipation of what comes as opposed to actually seeing what's arrived - because sometimes the thing that arrives comes as a complete surprise and it's completely unexpected.

A great example of that is when the broadcasters decided to put several cameras on the Accrington v Stevenage game on the last day of the season. Their decision to do so must have been based on their excited anticipation of automatic promotion celebrations at the Wham Stadium - instead of another ground which can be found just off Filton Avenue in Bristol.

I did laugh out loud when I saw the highlights programme. We got a few minutes of single camera coverage despite the result and the frenzy which ensued - whilst the Wham match highlights ran a lot longer and they were complimented with a commentator too. Oh well!

So back to three days after the Wombles match in December and we're at home to Leyton Orient. Gaffers scored our opener after he controlled a diagonal ball on his chest and weaved his way into the box before taking his time and netting a shot from eight yards on the half hour mark.

But the visitors equalised as the first half entered stoppage time to leave it one-one at half time and leave many of us toying with whether a Mars bar at the interval really was a good idea following the food frenzy of the previous three days - which is traditional in the western world in celebrating a famous birth.

So we thought about it and decided it would be nothing less than sheer gluttony to force a whole Mars bar into our still-bursting abdomens. And we thought the reasonable alternative was to share a Twix. And it was then that a moment of clarity hit me and it was just a wee bit bizarre!

Standing in the Blackthorn End - with two chocolate fingers in my hand - I realised that the truth of the clash between good and evil which exists between us and 'them down the road' was being subliminally screened to millions of viewers all around the world. It just seemed to hit me out of nowhere!

And when this awakening of truth happened - I would have fallen off my chair if I'd had one. But I was standing on the concrete steps in the North Terrace. So I thought it best to not fall over - because there's a group of young lads who stand not far from where I stand and they're pretty good at introducing impromptu songs in a split second and I really didn't want to feature in something like, "Ginge fell over! Ginge fell over!"

They're very good at what they do. I'd go as far as to say 'gifted'! And their own particular specialty is destroying - in song - each and every visiting goal keeper who - at some point - has to occupy the goal just yards from where they stand in front of the Blackthorn End.

Let's put it this way - you wouldn't want to get their attention in any way shape or form. So you don't really stand a chance if you're standing right in front of them while you're wearing neon yellow clothes and ridiculously big gloves. The inevitable is going to happen. We know it. The lads know it. And all keepers who we've just left behind in League Two know it too. And there's more chance of a Yeovil supporter appearing on Mastermind than there is a visiting goalkeeper to the Mem getting one over on these lads. And that's why I decided to not fall off the chair I didn't have!

So what was it that was revealed to me in this moment of clarity? Simple.

Star Wars - The Force Awakens was released in December and light sabers were everywhere. But it was the colours of the weapons in the film which grabbed my attention out of nowhere after I found myself staring down at two chocolate fingers and trying to decide which one was the smallest - so that I could give Helen the big finger. And that's when it happened.

It's not as if there was a Gashead who looks like an Ewok standing near me to ignite the thought. And I'm not even sure if Stu Sinclair was in the lineup for this particular match? Even then - he may be hairy but he's not as hairy as Chewbacca. So the realisation just came out of the blue. And that's what I'm referring to!

In the Star Wars films - the Forces of Good use blue light sabers and the Forces of Darkness use red ones.

I think what I'm trying to say is this - I think George Lucas is a Gashead! He knows the truth about the fight between good and evil along the banks of the Avon!

I know it sounds a bit random. But is it? Trust me - you'll never be able to watch these films in quite the same way ever again! And if Jabba the Hut makes a move from Wimbledon to 'them down the road' - you'll see I'm truly onto something!

So it was one-one at half time and the second half was about to kick off. The teams came out and the Leyton Orient keeper - dressed in neon yellow and wearing ridiculously big gloves - made his way onto the pitch and towards the Blackthorn End as the inevitable awaited to greet him. And both halves of our chocolate sensations disappeared as the second half began – but we only had to wait eight minutes to witness another kind of sensation.

Browner delivered a long ball from just inside our own half and was met by an Irishman at full speed - on the edge of the penalty box - who thundered a sublime left footed volley into the top right hand corner past Alex Cisak.

The keeper didn't stand a chance. It was incredible to watch and the celebrations which ensued will remain with me for a long time. And it was on that night that a certain song made its roaring debut at the Memorial Stadium and it's a song which I hope we'll enjoy singing for a few seasons to come…

"Oh Rory Gaffney you are the love of my life. Oh Rory Gaffney I'd let you shag my wife. Oh Rory Gaffney I want ginger hair too!"

There's something about celebrations after a goal. I'm convinced they're different. It's not unusual to go a bit 'mental' after the ball hits the back of the net - but for me there are different types of 'mental'.

There's the kind of 'mental' which happens after you see a goal being scored at a crucial point in a game after a decent bit of build-up play or even a set piece.

The Liam Lawrence free kick against Crawley Town at our ground in April is a great example. Nine yards outside the eighteen yard box and a stunning right foot strike into the top left hand corner. We could see the potential of a goal before he hit the ball. It was possible. He then hit it beautifully and we all went 'mental'. Great strike. Great goal. Great celebrations.

But what about the kind of celebrations which follow an incredible strike which is completely unexpected? That's what happened after Gaffers' volley against Orient.

It wasn't expected. It was a long ball from Browner and I don't think anyone expected Rory to hit it on the volley and that just took everyone by complete surprise and so the 'mental-ness' of the celebrations which ensued were courtesy of the total surprise at what we'd just witnessed!

It was a stunner. And there was more to come as our Ginger hit-man set his sights on Luton. Rory Gaffney had arrived and his announcement of his arrival was made for all to see and hear and sing as nine thousand voices filled the Mem with his song. And Shaun Derry heard it too!

4 YEAR THAT WAS, YEARS THAT WERE

They say you can tell a lot about a man based on three things and the trio of truth for blokes pertains to shoes, shoe size and pants.

And please don't ask me who 'they' are? I've been trying to find out for years and I'm quietly confident that I'm a good researcher into things. But to no avail...

Take the Pope not having a mobile phone etc. I mentioned my finding earlier when I wrote about trying to arrange a mass exorcism for 'them down the road'. That took some digging! But I've dug and dug over decades to be honest and the outcome remains that 'they' remain ever-elusive. And it's highly likely it will remain that way.

Shoes. Shoe size. Pants. And the reason why this is being introduced in a book about Bristol Rovers making club history at the end of the 2015/2016 season can be merited by certain events which took place on the final day of last year following an invitation I received to interview our gaffer and film his squad.

Now, before you start to get strange ideas - no it wasn't an invitation to film our gaffer and his squad in their shoes and pants. That would be ridiculous and there's no place for ridiculousness in this book. This is genuine...

What you're about to read may shock you. It's regarding one of our 'heart-throb' players and his choice of underwear. And I say 'heart-throb' based only on what I've heard said by female members of the Blue Army.

So the label is theirs - not mine. But don't get me wrong - I can see why Lee Mansell gets a fair bit of that kind of attention. He's a good looking bloke and I'm comfortable enough in my own sexuality to say that. No problem. It's just that he's not my type. I much prefer Bodin!

So how did it come to pass that I saw Mansell in his pants? Well, the truth is I didn't. But my partner Helen - the person responsible for me now being a Gashead - did see him wandering around in his underwear because she came with me to help out with the filming at the training session in Henbury. And this is what happened. Allegedly. Just added that to keep myself safe from libel!

The year's close was upon us and what a year it had been. And so it was on a Gashead high that I decided to produce a short 2015 review film to celebrate the incredible twelve months which were about to reach their conclusion.

The victorious May Promotion Final at Wembley saw us return to the Football League and our League Two campaign up until the final whistle against Orient had seen us play 24 games with 12 wins with eight matches lost and four drawn. And we were sitting sixth in the league table on forty points.

Have a wee think about that. Sixth place. That's not bad considering it hadn't been that long since we were doing battle on some Conference surfaces which looked more like what Neil Armstrong saw when he jumped out of his spaceship. Sixth. What an impressive bit of work by our lads and the gaffer! And what a great position it was to be in as we headed towards Auld Lang Syne!

Now I'd been filming and editing short productions about BRFC in my spare time since that infamous draw away to Dover towards the end of our non-league adventure and the films themselves had become popular and well received by Gasheads on several different social media platforms. So it just seemed right to produce something which captured 'the year that was' because I really felt that the events of 2015 merited such a production.

I began pulling together the footage and started the edit a few days before New Year's Eve and it was all going to plan. The structure of the piece was looking fine - but I felt that some new filming would help the piece along. So I drove across town towards the Mem to ask permission to get some shots of the stadium to use in the film. And when

I arrived - I met up with the club's press officer - Keith Brookman.

I explained to Keith what I was doing and he was fine with me filming at the ground. But then I thought it would be great to get some of the players or even the manager to do something on camera for the supporters?

So I asked Keith if it would be possible? He said that no one was around - but I was more than welcome to attend the Thursday press conference on New Year's Eve at The Lawns training ground. And with a massive smile on my face I replied, "Fantastic! Thank you very much!"

And that was that! And I was very grateful to Keith for his invite.

Most clubs tend to be very 'guarded' when it comes to outsiders requesting access of any kind. But my own experience of approaching lower league clubs is that they're very welcoming.

I first experienced this when I was working as a football producer at Scottish Television. I spent the latter part of a twelve year career in the sports department - mostly producing output which focussed on the Scottish Premier League and UEFA Champions League.

But in the late nineties - the company acquired to rights to broadcast matches from the Scottish Football League's First Division and I was asked if I would oversee the creation of a brand new football show? And to be honest - I was a bit apprehensive.

My unease was courtesy of no longer working on programming which included the likes of Celtic and Rangers and I wasn't sure if the move to the lower leagues would be a step down for my career. But my boss reassured me that my move wouldn't be considered a step down - that in fact it would be seen as a step up because I would have the responsibility of delivering a brand new football production. So I accepted.

It was the best move I ever made. Working alongside the first division clubs was a whole lot easier and a whole lot more fun than being involved with the premier sides. The lower league guys were so welcoming and accommodating to what I needed from them for the new production. And they more or less told me I could send cameras at any time and to film or interview whoever I needed. For the programme, They were incredible! And Bristol Rovers are exactly the same!

The new programme was launched and I called it Football First. Within a year it attracted sponsorship from Bell's whisky because of the viewing figures. And that's when the serious lunches began...

Now, I was no stranger to the occasional boozy lunch in the late nineties. In fact - that happened every day. Football journalism and drinking went hand in hand in those days and it wasn't uncommon to indulge in a three course lunch which involved a starter of lager, a main course of lager and a large red wine for dessert.

We all worked hard and we played a lot harder. I wish I could tell you all about what I saw and did - but there are many well-known faces who remain in the game and in football broadcasting and I'm currently not in a financial position to end up in court.

Crazy days and crazier nights. The perfect life for a young man in his thirties. So really - when I think back on it all now - it's really not a surprise that I ended up in residential rehab ten years later. And to be honest - looking at where I am now in my life - I really wouldn't have it any other way.

Now that's what's known - in television speak - as a teaser. I did mention earlier about my past and whether or not I'd reveal more in this book. And there you have it. It has begun. But I'll get into the grimness of that particular episode in my life a little bit later on.

And it's by no means a gratuitous insert into this book about our club. To be honest - if it hadn't been for my struggle with the booze then I wouldn't have ended up in this part of the country and I'd never have met Helen and so I'd never have been taken to the Mem in 2013 and I'd never have ended up at Wembley to witness Mansell's (I haven't forgotten the pants story) penalty which saw DC sprinting across the pitch and I'd most certainly wouldn't have been standing in the Blackthorn End when Browner tapped it in with his right foot which caused bedlam and I'd have completely missed watching Wael being held aloft down Gloucester Road towards the Queen Vic to the sounds of "We've got our Rovers back!"

Oh no! Nothing gratuitous at all! I'm grateful to the illness. My whole life changed when I came into recovery six years ago and a massive part of my new life was being introduced to the supporters of the blue and white quarters when I settled in Bristol – the city which I know in my heart will now always be my home.

I don't dwell on the past these days. But I remember past days and those days which are now no more were days which were to push me towards following the Gas. Those past experiences of producing programming about the lower leagues in Scotland were what drew me to the north terrace. So they're very relevant to me and my story.

So I hope you don't mind me sharing all of this with you - but there's a powerful connection between that time in my life and what inspired me to begin to evolve into a Gashead. It took a bit of time…

I remember going to my first match at the Mem in the spring of 2013. Helen and I had only been seeing one another for six months and she is a total Gashead. Proper like!

Helen hadn't been going to games for a few seasons due to personal circumstances and it was on that sunny spring day that she suggested we go to a match?

I thought it was a great idea because I'd been focussing on other aspects of my life too for a few years and had therefore been away from football entirely. So we headed up to the Mem and I remember I wasn't really that impressed with what I saw happening on the pitch. But there was something that did grab my attention from where we were standing on the east terrace - and that something was what I saw and heard coming from the Blackthorn End.

I'll never forget that feeling and it was that feeling which re-awakened so many incredible memories from my time producing Football First.

It was the sheer rawness of what was going on which pulled me towards returning again and again and I knew exactly why I kept returning to Filton Ave and eventually awakened to the truth that I'd fallen in love with our club - an awakening which was to take place away to Dover in the penultimate fixture of our non-league campaign two years later.

So, as you know, we ended up at Wembley in May 2015 and Ellis netted the equaliser and Mansell did something a wee bit special during the penalty shoot-out. But how did I end up there?

Relegation the year previously saw me see so much anguish at our ground on that day and that was when I made a decision. I suppose I was a supporter but I wouldn't have called myself a Gashead. To me there's a difference.

In my own humble opinion - a supporter goes to the match and then goes home and carries on with their usual Saturday night as if nothing has happened. Maybe a bit happy or maybe a bit down? And there's absolutely nothing wrong with that. Nothing!

A Gashead - on the other hand - goes to the match and then returns home either in some kind of state of grace -or a dribbling emotional wreck. The latter applies to me. Helen too. And I've noticed something else…

It was in the autumn of last year that I went to visit my family on the east coast near Felixstowe. I only spent a few days and I had to arrive back to Bristol on a Saturday.

Now this was a first for me and it was probably a first because it's unusual for me to be anywhere but close to our city on match days – unless we're on the road to an away game.

It just didn't cross my mind. Nothing unusual for me to be honest. And I jumped into my car at around 2pm as I waved goodbye to my folks – with the full intention of enjoying listening to our game on the radio as I sped back to Avon.

The terror which hit me when I realised I couldn't receive BBC Radio Bristol - once I was on the road – scared the living daylights out of me. And once the terror had subsided - about an hour later - I found myself driving in anguish in full knowledge and acceptance that I'd be denied match coverage. Needless to say – I broke the sound barrier to get to just past Swindon. But please don't tell the cops!

So I was a supporter on the day we got relegated in 2014 - but a wee voice within me said, *"You'll follow them next season and you'll do everything you can to support them and the others around you and play your own small part in doing the very best you can to get right behind the team and cheer and scream and shout until they find their way back to the Football League!"*

And that's what I did. And our Conference campaign was one of the best experiences I've ever had. That's why I wrote *Faithful and True - A Gashead's Story.*

The connection between my past and what happened on the 3rd of May 2014 took place on Strathmore Road – just around the corner from the Memorial Stadium – as we all walked away and Helen and so many others were in tears.

I said something to her which I hoped would help ease the pain. I knew one of two things would happen after I said it. It would either involve her agreeing or I would end up with a sore face.

I told Helen about Hibernian FC and how they were relegated in the late nineties from the Scottish Premier League and fell into the Scottish First Division. And with that - the coverage of their season in the second tier was to feature on *Football First*.

I shared about how Hibs went down – but how they got rid of players who weren't playing for the shirt and how they found a unity which saw them win promotion back to the SPL the following year. Sound familiar?

Helen didn't dislocate my jaw. Instead – she agreed and we only had ourselves to blame. And that maybe we had to go down to find something we'd lost - something which would re-ignite the club? And as you know - we ended up finding that something and a helluva lot more!

So it was at that time when I was seeing and hearing what was going on on the steps of the north stand that I was reminded of working alongside the lower league clubs in Scotland during times which were very fulfilling for me. And that's how the initial connection between me and the Rovers happened. Real people being affected by real football.

For me - supporters of the lower league sides have so much in common.

We compete against one another and on occasions - we hate one another. But the one thing we share with one another is the love and passion we have for the club which represents the town or city in which we live or from where we hail from.

We represent the very life and lives which can be found and seen and heard within and around the streets and alleyways which spring forth from the turf and stands and terraces of the grounds which we hold close to our own hearts. And it's within these streets and alleyways where love and loss can be found - the loves and losses which anchor our experience of life to the pavements and pathways in times of laughter or hurt.

Whether we smile or whether we cry - it's in the places which the pavements and pathways caress where we're held in celebration or in comfort because that's what home does.

Home is simply there when we need it to be and it's within this home that the hurt and joy of life reaches out - onto the pavements and pathways which touch the streets and alleyways which embrace the turf and the stands and the terracing which is also our home.

And so we feel blessed. Blissful in knowing that all that this is isn't just about ninety minutes of football. It's about the lives of thousands of families represented and coming together to stand together and support one another in times of further elation and sometimes sorrow. Football isn't just a game. Football is everything that a family is - especially togetherness.

What's happening at home makes us laugh louder or feel the pain of loss much harder. The right result can lift the home which lays beyond the ground. The wrong result can help to put other aspects of life into perspective.

Highs and lows. But much better to have the highs and lows than be without the warmth and expectation which each new Sunday brings. Each day from that day a day of two halves – the humdrum of everyday living being spurred forward by the anticipation of what Saturday may bring.

We feel it because we care. And we care because we love. And if you have those two lives in your life - then you're living a life of full.

It's not just about football. Well, it isn't for me. Of course the game is paramount and I love watching matches whether were at home or on the road. I also love knowing more about the manager and his squad. I'd love to know more and I'd love to know more because they're the ones out there giving it all for ninety minutes. And that time is an experience filled with highs and lows which I will take home with me. They're part of our lives. We talk about all of them in our house and that means they're in our home. And we care about them just as much as we care about the results at the final whistle.

For Helen and me - there's a wholeness to the experience of being a football supporter. And that totality is quite complex as it unifies so many different aspects of our lives - a unity which I'm truly grateful to have now in my life.

Despite my own personal history with football production - the way I now feel about the game and our club something very new. I worked in football for so many years – but the way I feel about it all now is something very new and very special to me.

I produced *Football First* for several years and I can honestly say they were the best and happiest broadcast years of my production career. It was nothing less than a riot!

The programme was presented by Jim Delahunt with two regular studio pundits. One was Andy Walker - former Celtic, Bolton Wanderers and Sheffield United striker. And the second studio analyst was Derek Johnstone - former Rangers and Chelsea player.

But the departure of Jim White from Scottish Television to Sky saw an increased workload for Jim - so I was on the lookout for a new presenter for Football First.

We were all genuinely gutted to see Jim White leave the Cowcaddens studios in the centre of Glasgow.

And when he departed - he took with him the greatest ever question to be put by a football journalist to a footballer of the highest distinction.

Brian Laudrup was a vital part of the Rangers team which dominated the Scottish Premier Division in the 1990s - winning three championships and scoring thirty three goals in one hundred and sixteen appearances for the Gers between 1994 and 1998. He won the Danish Footballer of the Year a record four times and made eighty two appearances - scoring twenty one goals - for Denmark and was named the fifth best player in the world by FIFA in 1992. Not bad!

The interview took place outside in a sunny setting near Glasgow in 1995 and it followed Laudrup's first season with Walter Smith's side.

And it was in this place - at this time - that Jim delivered the question which no other football journo had the balls to ask, *"How come you are so good?"*

Now I have to say - I mean no disrespect to Whitey (no one calls him Jim in Glasgow) because I've worked with him and he's a lovely, funny bloke and we both produced the Scotsport Review of the Year 1997 together and it went down a storm. But that question is still being discussed along the banks of the Clyde and harbourside in Nyhavn.

It was bad. Fair enough. But to be honest - I think Whitey missed a great opportunity to defuse the situation. I reckon he should've snogged Laudrup after putting the question to him. In for a penny in for a pound and all that!

When it comes to journos and questions to managers - there's one which still leaves me stunned. I hear it all the time from broadcasters on the radio and television for years and it just doesn't make any sense?

"Great win for you today! You must be delighted?"

Darrell - if you're reading this right now - I'll give you a hundred quid if you answer that question with this:

"Delighted? No. Not really. Actually - I'm gutted!

I was hoping we'd lose today. But we ended up winning.

There's more to a game than just scoring lots of goals and getting three points. It's about taking part and I just don't feel we took part for most of today's match.

Sure we hit the back of the net on several occasions - but the togetherness was all over the place. We were drifting apart for long periods in the game. We need to focus on that during training over the next couple of days!"

Why on earth would you ask someone if they're delighted when they clearly are delighted?

It's exactly the same when you get out of the shower - wrap a towel around you to hide the scary bits - walk down the hallway and into the bedroom and smash your little toe into one of the legs of the bed! And then someone who's supposed to love you asks, *"Was that sore?"*

Of course it's fucking sore! Why the fuck wouldn't it be sore? And why the fuck wouldn't a football manager be delighted after winning a game?

You don't need to ask him if he is? Ask him something else! Just keep it simple like, *"Darrell. Well done!"* And then point the mic at him! Trust me - he knows what to say! Rant over!

So where was I? Oh yes. Lee Mansell in his pants! But you'll have to wait a little bit longer. I need to finish with the Football First bit first. I promise it'll be worth the wait!

To be fair - interviewing managers and players isn't as easy as you might think. It's not that it's difficult - it's more like you're sometimes up against the personification of 'bipolar'.

Highs and lows. Wins and defeats.

Without stating the obvious - winning gaffers are straightforward. You just ask them if they're delighted and why they think they're players are so good? But managers who've just lost a match can be a bit of a struggle because you know they don't really want to be standing in front you with a mic and camera plonked in front of them as you record them looking gutted for the whole world to see.

In many ways - for the likes of you and me to understand - it's probably the same scenario as standing on Weston pier as you're minding your own business and eating an ice cream and a seagull takes a giant dump on your head. And as you stand in horror and disbelief - in the moments before you realise you could be in for some life changing luck - a stranger with a mic and another stranger with a camera assault you with, "You can't be delighted? Can you?"

So I was always very careful with managers who'd just been on the receiving end of a dumping. Then again - I never really interviewed that many players and gaffers.

As a producer - my role was to oversee the production from the studios. So I spent most of my time working on the programme running order at my desk or in a dark edit suite somewhere in the bowels of the building.

The reporters were to ones who I dressed in full body armour and sent to the games to speak to the players and playing staff after a matches. But I've interviewed a few in my time - and the scariest was a certain Dutchman who was infamous for his trackside ranting and cold steely stare.

Dick Advocaat replaced Walter Smith as Rangers manager in 1998 and he was a no nonsense kind of guy. But beneath his furious exterior - I'd always been convinced that deep, deep down inside - there could be found a furious interior.

And it was towards that fury that I was sent on a day when our reporter pool was decimated by a diarrhoea outbreak and the journalist allocated to the Rangers match phoned in sick from his toilet. And I remember feeling really gutted for him. Not because he was ill - but instead - he was doing exactly the same at home as he would be doing in the tunnel at Ibrox after the game as he waited for Dick. Shitting himself!

So we had a problem. My responsibility at this time was with *Football First* - not the premier division programme. But the producer of that production was frantically trying to get a replacement to cover the Rangers match - but it wasn't happening.

The chances are that all the reporters had been out together on the booze the night before and had ended up in some dodgy kebab shop at 3am after being asked to leave a certain 'sticky carpet' nightclub because they were scaring the regulars - regulars which included Eastern European sailors and Glasgow crime lords.

Now this kind of behaviour by the reporters wasn't unusual. I know this for sure because I was usually out with them. But what was unusual was that they hadn't been able to make it into work. That was very odd.

Our reporters were and remain a hardy bunch and the only events which could stop them from going to a match were either an atomic blast or the promise of a shag. So we were pretty much guaranteed that they'd end up at the ground where they were allocated to be.

But on that morning - it came to pass that they were nowhere to be seen - but could be heard if you stood outside their bathrooms.

So we had to improvise. Producer number one selected a game to cover and I was allocated the remaining fixture. Ibrox. And that's when I felt as if I'd suddenly caught what the reporters had because I had to run to the gents.

Rangers won and I've never been so relieved in my whole life. And that's quite an incredible thing to admit to - because in those days I was a Celtic supporter!

So I was standing pitch side after the game with the cameraman - not far from the tunnel. And it was from that particular entrance of darkness that he emerged. Advocaat. And the look on his face was what you'd expect from him after an impressive win. He looked furious.

The radio lad was interviewing him first because they were still live on air - so I had to wait a few minutes. And it was the longest two hundred seconds I've ever had to endure.

At one point I looked at my cameraman and he returned my empty gaze with, "Rather you than me!"

I did think about falling on a sword. But all I had was a big fluffy microphone. The other alternative was to burst into a loud rendition of the 'Fields of Athenry' - very popular at Celtic and absolutely guaranteed to provide me with a sudden ending within the red brick walls of Ibrox.

But alas. I'd run out of time because the radio guy had run out of live air time and he'd finished with Dutch. And Dutch began making his way towards me...

We packed the kit into the crew car once we were finished and headed back to the studios. I then arrived back at my desk and handed the interview tape to the sports assistant whose job it was to watch all interviews and log them before they were sent to the edit suites to be added onto the edited match highlights.

She took the tape and wandered into the viewing room to view the interview as I sat down and began working on my own programme running order - still unable to talk about what had happened.

It was only about five minutes later when I felt someone standing next to me and I looked up to see her standing looking down at me - eyes wide open. And then she did something remarkable. She managed to say something even though her jaw was still hitting the floor, "What the fuck did you do?"

To be honest - I didn't really know how to answer that question because what had happened during the interview still felt dreamlike in its surreal memory in my mind. All I could say was, "I don't know. It just happened. I didn't do anything and I didn't say anything before I asked him if he was delighted with the result? It just happened!"

The Rangers manager - Dick Advocaat - had smiled.

The Dutchman had taken his position in front of the camera as he looked down at his feet. Then, he looked up and his eyes met mine and then he smiled. A nice big happy smile beneath the cold blue windows to his soul. And it was at that point that I knew how Clarice Starling felt in *Silence of the Lambs!*

Advocaat's steely blue gaze pierced my eyeballs as he answered my questions and I was thrown completely off guard by his demeanour. He was happy and that scared the shit out of me! And it was to leave me and my colleagues baffled for a long, long time.

In all honesty - it was one of the best several minutes I ever enjoyed in telly. Sometimes fear can be fun.

He was brilliant. But I did have the feeling that his joy was courtesy of him remembering that he'd forgotten to rip someone's head off in the dressing room - as if the imminence of him wreaking havoc on some poor player bestowed him with a welcome and unexpected joy. And as for me - I was delighted because I wasn't that player.

Dressing rooms. I've only ever been in one when it's been full of players either before or during or after a game. And I'd love to be in one at half time to hear what's being said - especially when the team's losing.

I suppose it all depends on the gaffer. I'm sure some throw things around - like towels, boots, shin pads and small players. But does that approach really work?

A good mate of mine up in Glasgow is a football writer for the Daily Record - arguably Scotland's most popular newspaper. Tony Haggerty is a lovely bloke and he's in the know regarding everything there is to know about the game up north and beyond.

With the departure of Jim White to Sky - former Rangers star Derek Johnstone was plonked into the presenter's chair and that meant I needed another pundit to sit alongside former Celtic striker Andy Walker for the match analysis. Cue Tony…

He was perfect. I'd met him a few times at the player/manager of the month awards lunches and he was impressive with his insight into the game. He was also young and good looking - not that age was important.

So with that I invited young Haggerty to join us on the programme and he was brilliant. He delivered an edgy look and feel which accompanied his views on the weekend's games. And it was when we came off air one Sunday afternoon - that he shared a certain dressing room story which had taken place during a match the previous week.

Now, when it comes to sweary words - the Scots do things a bit differently. We don't just swear. Swearing comes from a deeply personal space within us.

When we deliver an outburst of expletives - it's as if the words come from such an intimate inner realm and they never really explode forth in sound. It's almost as if the word is delivered under breath to the point it's almost not heard. Swearing really means a lot to us - so it's as if we're extremely reticent to let the words go - even though it's more important that we use them! And they're a bit different up north too.

The usual suspects remain the same. But we do have our own replacements for the universally accepted words which can be found and used in every corner of the globe. For example - in Scotland, 'Fud' replaces 'Bellend' and 'Twat' is replaced with 'Fanny'! Get it? Good!

So let's give this a go. In Bristol - you might hear, "That bellend is a right twat!" However, in Glasgow you're more likely to hear, "That fud is a right fanny!"

So Tony was telling me about the dressing room incident and it's brilliant. And the outcome of what happened probably had a much better effect in getting the players to get their arses into gear!

He's affectionately known as 'Yogi' north of the border and he served with the likes of Swansea, Celtic, Hibs and Falkirk.

John Hughes - an imposing central defender in his time and none the less after he hung up his boots - was to enjoy a managerial spell with Falkirk and it was while he was gaffer with the Bairns that the dressing room incident took place.

Half time. Falkirk are losing and Yogi decides to read the riot act to his squad - a squad which included Portuguese centre forward Pedro Moutinho. And it was Pedro who revealed the truth of what happened during that interval to Tony. This is an exclusive for Bristol!

Yogi is drilling each and every player individually. Shouting and pointing at them one by one and screaming, *"How about you, you c..t - what are you up to? The TV cameras are here! You can't hide!"*

All the players were getting it in the neck and then it was Moutinho's turn. Hughes pointed at him and shouted, *"Pedro! Aye! You! What's Portuguese for fanny?!"* To which Pedro replied, *"Yogi!"*

Moutinho assured Tony that bedlam ensued. However – Tony remains uncertain as to what kind of bedlam was to ensue. It may have been that everyone burst out laughing and that inspired them to get the job done. Or - Yogi decided to throw all his players out of the window. We'll never know!

So from a dressing room in Falkirk to just outside a dressing room at *The Lawns* training ground in Bristol on a sunny winter's New Year's Eve where I was filming for an end of year review of our successes during 2015.

It's at this venue where the press conference takes place every Thursday before each Bristol Rovers match and I'd been invited along by the club's press officer - Keith Brookman.

Helen was with me and everyone there couldn't have been more welcoming. I just needed a quick interview with Darrell to drop into the edit and I asked Keith if it would be okay to speak to a few of the players too. And he said it would be no problem at all. In fact - it was his idea to get all of the players together to do an en-mass *"Happy New Year"* to the camera to include at the end of the film.

The interview with Darrell went well and I asked him about what was going through his mind when he ran across the pitch at Wembley towards thousands of Gasheads just after Mansell netted the penalty? This was his answer:

"Hopefully not pulling a hamstring! Just to share in front of thousands of our supporters that had been through hell. We'd hit rock bottom as a football club and to see the relief on everyone's faces to get out at the first time of asking is something that will stay with me!"

He was and is a gentleman and it was a pleasure to meet him. And then we were directed outside to set up the camera for the shot of all the players wishing all the Gasheads a Happy New Year. And that's when it happened!

I didn't see it. I was getting the camera ready and the players were emerging from the dressing room to start training and I had my back to the door.

I looked up and saw a look of mixed emotions on Helen's face. The first expression was one of pure joy. The second was one of pure dismay. And that's the best way I can describe what I saw.

Have you ever seen someone heightened by mixed emotions? Up until that moment - I thought I had. But I really hadn't. And I truly hadn't because I saw it for real for the first time as she looked over my shoulder towards the door of the dressing room with a look of lust and lament!

I didn't even bother to turn around. I was too fixated with the expression on her face. I'd never seen anything like it before. Well, that's not strictly true. I'd seen one half of the two looks and I see it a lot. She looked like she was having an orgasm while eating a lemon!

And yes - we're quite a fruity family!

Now, this expression went on for a while. I just stood and watched her watch whatever or whoever she was watching. Then it stopped and I was half expecting her to light up a cigarette. And that would have been odd because she doesn't smoke!

So I asked her, *"Are you okay?"* And she just looked at me in a kind of half-spent, half sorrowful way and replied, *"I've just seen Mansell in his pants!"*

Now, I wouldn't have thought that would have been a visual image which would leave a woman a bit confused on the feelings front? And I'm sure a few blokes wouldn't mind seeing him in his pants either? So I was a wee bit baffled as to why Helen was gyrating and grimacing at the same time? So I said, *"And?"*

And she replied, *"He's wearing baggy grey pants! He looks like he's in a nappy!"*

Let's be honest. I reckon Mansell can wear what he wants after that Wembley penalty. Helen agrees. But I think she's still considering sending him a triple pack of tight black boxers in her own small way to say thank you!

The filming was a huge success and the lads gathered together in front of the camera and delivered a big and loud *"Happy New Year!"* for all Bristol Rovers supporters. And they really are a fantastic bunch of players.

2015 had been an incredible year. And as the final edit was completed and the film was uploaded onto YouTube - I had no idea that it would receive so many views within the few hours prior to the midnight bells tolling the arrival of another time. And I had absolutely no clue that 2016 would herald a day which many now regard as one of the most important days in the history of Bristol Rovers!

Bristol Rovers 2 v 0 Luton

2nd January 2016

Darrell Clarke's men clinch a win in their opening match of the new year after on loan striker Rory Gaffney scores twice in his second successive game.

Rovers climb above Wycombe into fifth in League Two and the Irish striker returns to his home club.

5 WE'LL MEET AGAIN

Rory Gaffney was recalled to Cambridge United at the start of January and there was an uneasy feeling amongst Rovers supporters.

We'd been hoping for and calling for a striker who was strong up front and he'd arrived in November. His spell at the Memorial Stadium was a short one - but long enough for him to become a massive hit with the supporters. Me included! And not just because he's one of our own - a ginger like me!

He'd become a favourite and he was going to be missed. A lot. It really didn't feel good when he left the club and with him no longer around - it meant that we couldn't let him know out loud that it was okay to shag our wives.

I was always quite happy to sing. I'm not married.

His departure wasn't exactly a surprise. Business is business and it was highly unlikely that Cambridge United were just going to extend his loan period when it was clear for all to see that the man from County Galway had slotted right into Clarke's squad and scored five goals during his short stay. So he had a lot to offer and what he had to offer was worth something.

Taylor had definitely found his form again - but was that to do with the arrival of his new partner up front in the shape of the on loan Irishman who was now no longer with us?

No disrespect to Matty. That's not my intention at all as I write these words. This was the time of Matty beginning to find his game again and his League Two Player of the Month nomination for December was testament to his performances on the pitch. I'm simply saying that Taylor and Gaffney were working so well together up front and one half of that striking duo was heading back to his home club.

I wasn't happy about seeing him leave the Mem. But I had and always will have complete faith and belief in our manager and his squad.

I wrote the following words the day before our away game to Barnet in January. It was our first match following the departure of the man who scored that incredible volley against Leyton Orient and who then went on to net another double against Luton in our opening match of 2016 - a match which saw us emerge 2-0 winners at home and sitting fifth on 43 points. This is what I wrote before we headed to the Hive:

'You feel it and you feel it long before the game even kicks off.

You feel it before the day of the match begins and it feels good to sense the calmness embrace you after days of speculation and anxiety surrounding whether or not a certain on-loan player will return to your club - because when he was with your team for just a short period of time he provided that 'something' up front which you and thousands of other Gashead faithful had been yearning for for so long.

But he's gone. And yet the calmness descends on the day before your away game and that's when you realise that what happens tomorrow is about a club and a team and supporters like no other.

Tomorrow isn't just about the absence of a certain striker. The day that comes is about history and passion and fight coming together in a time of recent success - which has seen your manager and one of your strikers nominated for December honours. And for all the right reasons because the blue and white that you adorn with pride has sung in song for weeks now and you're beginning to think that 'something special' is beginning to take shape and you now know you're not the only one feeling this feeling. And you realise that maybe the departure of that certain player - back to his home club - was some kind of fate which will reveal itself in the weeks and months which come.

Maybe you'll see fate do what fate does best?

Maybe it's already been decided by the Gods of the Beautiful Game? Maybe the script has already been written and it doesn't matter who leaves and who arrives? Maybe your club's destiny has awakened and you're about to witness something very special in the final half of the season. And you think, "Why not?" No man a team makes - with the exception of your manager!

And still the calmness holds you close - following days of feeling unsettled - as the night blackens in preparation for what the dawn day will bring. And if there's one thing you know it's this - you won't be alone on your travels. You'll be part of a Blue Army which will descend on them and you will all do what you all do best - you will show those who you all descend upon that Irene's awakening wasn't that day at Wembley. Her awakening was when she was sent down all those months before and her awakening was to spark because you and all in blue and white followed her into the abyss where you sang and chanted her return to her rightful place.

Tomorrow sees the awakening continue. And fear you they should - because no one man this team makes. This team is a brotherhood and this club is a family like no other. And we stay 'til the end. Always the end!'

6 BULLY BEES

BARNET 1 V BRISTOL ROVERS 0
9TH JANUARY 2016

We were heading to the Hive and I wasn't exactly buzzing.
London traffic does my head in but it was all part of the
adventure in the immediate aftermath of Gaffers. But there
was something to look forward to after the A5 and the
Nightmare on Honeypot Lane. Yes, you read correctly.
Nightmare traffic on Honeypot Lane as we headed to the
Hive to play the Bees. You couldn't make this fucking stuff
up!

So our 'something to look forward to came in the shape of
Liam Lawrence who had just signed from Shrewsbury
Town and that gave us a wee bit of solace following the

trauma of losing Rory. To be honest - I had faith in the team - but I was miserable. Then again - I am Scottish!

This is really weird - because as I'm writing these words - I'm sinking into a foul mood as I remember back to that freezing Saturday and everything that was happening around the game. I just felt gutted to be honest and I'm actually feeling gutted all over again.

There were lots of rumours flying around as always regarding his possible return - but you can never truly believe anything you hear until you see it happening for real with your own eyes.

It's exactly the same with the Matty Taylor 'will he stay or will he go' rumours which are currently bombarding social media. And as it stands right now - no one knows. But there are plenty of rumours abounding at the moment and one of them is regarding him moving to - of all places - Hearts in Edinburgh?

Now this particular rumour has been doing the rounds for quite some time now and I just can't see him heading up there for one reason and one reason only. And it has absolutely nothing to do with the fact that it would be a move to Scottish Football.

Now don't get me wrong - with the exception of the Old Firm - Scottish football can be a bit dreary. Then again – watching Hibs win the Scottish Cup Final for the first time in one hundred and fourteen years is hardly an uninspiring spectacle. And even though they lost - I'm sure the Rangers players found it all a bit 'heightening' too - albeit their 'high' was probably thanks to adrenalin as they saw twenty thousand Hibee pitch invasion hurtling towards them at five hundred miles an hour.

But that kind of excitement in Scottish football is quite rare. But not as rare as finding a Hibs supporter who remembers winning the Scottish Cup in 1902.

Now all this is coming from me - a proud Scot! But I'm serious when I say it wouldn't be an exciting move for Taylor - unless he thinks being pummelled by eight foot defenders in sub-zero temperatures in an Edinburgh Derby as the sound of the Proclaimers singing *'My heart was broken'* is an experience which excites him? I doubt he does - because it wouldn't be his heart that gets broken. Big Scottish defenders prefer breaking bones - then wind. But not always in that order!

No. I can't see Taylor going to Hearts. And it's got nothing to do with psycho opposition defenders or anything else to do with football. It's more to do with staying alive. And I'm not referring to the Beegees!

You see, Tynecastle Stadium is the home of Heart of Midlothian FC and it can be found in the Gorgie area of Edinburgh. The supporters refer to themselves as 'Jambos' and this nickname is derived from them also being known as the 'Jam Tarts'. And in my own humble opinion - not the best name for football supporters but an absolute winner for a bakery which is staffed by swingers.

Once a prosperous area for breweries - that prosperity has now disappeared and all that can be found in Gorgie is a high school, a community farm and an entire population still scared shitless Jambos following a lethal outbreak of Legionaires Disease in 2012. Yippee!

When that happened - the locals tried to escape and it looked like a mass exodus version of the opening title sequence from 'Trainspotting'!

Then there's the language barrier? If you think it's difficult to understand someone from Glasgow - try someone from Gorgie!

I'm serious - you could be walking down the street minding your own business in the vicinity of Tynecastle and someone could walk up to you and start talking to you and you'd be completely none the wiser as to what you're being told.

They could be saying anything from:

"The castle isn't here - it's up the posh part of town" to *"Do you know where the nearest chemist is because I think my Legionaires is back?"* to *"I'm going to cut your head off and fuck your skull!"*

You wouldn't know any better. Trust me. I've been there. I've heard them. I heard them and I didn't have a clue. There's more chance of 'them down the road' witnessing ninety minutes of football than Taylor having a conversation in Gorgie.

It's also very important to note that Gorgie can be found in Edinburgh. It's a city steeped in history and a history which gave birth to Sir Arthur Conan Doyle and Sherlock Holmes investigating crimes most foul; body snatchers and witch trials. It's a bit like Yeovil - but without the banjos.

Nope. Matty should stay with us for a while longer. It was his debut entry into the Football League and I reckon a few more seasons and he'll be ready to ply his trade elsewhere.

There's no rush and why on earth would he want to sign for a club with not a lot of silverware to choose from and where death and madness and plague and incoherence lurks around every street corner and alleyway?

But back to that sweet Saturday near Honeypot Lane where we knew Barnet would be a difficult game and we expected to get bundled about a bit.

The Bees' two previous matches were away to Northampton and Cambridge and they'd been beaten on both occasions. But we knew they weren't going to be a walkover at home by any means with Martin Allen's men having secured seven home wins out of their opening twelve.

They may have been sitting eighteenth in the table on twenty eight points - but the Hive is always a difficult encounter because it's more akin to a hornets nest.

So we arrived at the Camrose Avenue ground and the weather was still awful. It was cold and it was drizzly and it pretty much summed up our mood following the departure of Gaffers.

But you follow - don't you? You just keep going and you just end up attracting a lot of hope to yourself at these times as a football supporter and it's just the way it is. Head down. Eyes front. Bovril and a Twix.

For me - I don't tend to look back a lot. I know a lot of supporters do that and that's fair enough. But I've never really seen the point in looking back - especially at results - and saying, *"What if?"*

It's pointless. It happened. Move on. But to be honest - I was worried heading to London for this game. It was as if all our prayers had been answered with the arrival of the man who ended up on the receiving end of invitations to break wedding vows. And then our answer was gone.

So we wander into the ground and I have to say - it's quit a nice ground. And if you have a fetish for tin - you'll find it hard leaving!

Love shack aside - we stroll in and our chairman is the first person we see. He's standing at the entrance to the VIP entrance and it's with much surprise that I notice he's not being mobbed by Gasheads asking the question, *"Are you doing a deal to get Gaffney back?"*

So Nick's standing there and he's looking quite calm and collected and I was really happy for him because it must be nothing short of a living nighmare sometimes when you've got people constantly approaching you and asking you the same question again and again and again.

Now, Helen knows Nick Higgs from a few years ago when she used to enjoy watching some of the matches at the Mem from one of the hospitality boxes. And she's always held him in high regard. So with that, we both stomped up to him and asked, *"Are you doing a deal to get Gaffney back?"*

With that, Higgs raises his hands and replies, *"We're talking to them. That's all I can say at the moment. And we're meeting with them this coming week!"*

Fair enough we thought. And so we chatted for a wee while longer and the three of us agreed it would be a hard, physical game ahead and a draw wouldn't be a bad result considering the way the home side treat visitors.

By this point - a group had gathered around us and everyone was waiting for their own turn to put the question to the chairman. So we decided to bumble along and head off to find a spot on the steps of the allocated away end as the icy drizzle began to fall once again in the hour before the fight started. And as the distance between ourselves and our chairman grew and grew – we found he disappeared in time amid the fading sound of, *"Are you doing a deal to get Gaffney back? Are you doing a deal to get Gaffney back?"*

And our conversation with Nick turned out to be a bit prophetic. It wasn't a match. It turned out to be a fight!

But there was a fight before the referee blew his whistle to start the match. There was the battle to get a hot drink before the game began.

We'd arrived fairly early so getting a decent spot to watch the 'skirmish' was taken care of quite easily - so all that was needed was something warm to eat and drink so as to avoid hypothermia or death by exposure.

So I departed our spot to hunt down some steaming solace from the food hut which was bolted onto the back of the away end of the tin Love Shack which was the arena for our entertainment for a few hours - and what I was see left me remembering how just good an actor Christian Bale is!

Exodus. Released twelve months earlier in cinemas across the land - it tells the story of Moses and how he led his people out of captivity in Egypt.

I'm sure you're familiar with the biblical adventure and I'm also sure you're wondering what the hell does pharaohs and baskets and dividing of a sea have to do with a League Two football clash between Barnet and the mighty Bristol Rovers?

Well, you see - it was impossible not to think of some kind of Exodus when I saw the length of the queue to get served from the small tin shack which was bolted to the back of the big tin shack!

Now, whenever I'm faced with any situation which leaves me a wee bit unhappy (especially when the temperatures are sub-zero and my favourite ginger striker has loved me and left me) my retort tends to always be the same, "Oh, for fuck's sake!"

I tend not to be a patient man. I've tried. I've tried hard on many different occasions in my life and to no avail. So I just stopped trying. I don't have the patience to practice being patient. And my intolerance for poor forward planning is something which fuels my impatience to the point where I wish I could stomp up and down. But I can't do that. I've only got one leg and there was this one time (not band camp) when I stomped up and down and my prosthetic leg flew off!

So I'm standing in the Exodus and I'm standing at the back and the Exodus isn't moving - which completely contradicts the meaning of Exodus.

It took forever. At one point I thought I might get lucky and see the second half. But slowly and surely - it didn't move a fucking inch.

At one point I actually walked to the front of the queue to see what was happening? Hold on - that's not right. I'll write that bit again. Here goes - at one point I actually walked to the front of the queue to see what wasn't happening? And what I saw left me speechless!

Now, bare in mind we sold out our allocation of tickets. We mobbed them as we always do. Best away support in the league by far as far as I'm concerned. Proud to be a Gashead. Especially proud to be a Gashead on the road. So we swarmed the Hive and the best they could do was put two - yes two - spotty teenagers on the frontline of serving hot food and drink to an entire army of blue.

And what left me speechless was that only Beavis seemed to be serving food - because Butthead was in charge of pushing the buttons on the till. And he was pushing the buttons in a way to suggest he was expecting the buttons to bite him. And I stood staring at him in that aghast way that you do - mouth open and soul destroyed - whilst wishing I was a button! Albeit a frozen button!

I was an almost empty shell of a man when Beavis eventually handed me two Bovrils and a Twix following a span of time which I'm convinced included an eclipse. I was going to say something but didn't want the hassle of having to appear before a ChildLine panel - so I just took it all and stumbled back to Helen - just in time to buy a half time draw ticket. Just one. Not two as I usually do at the Mem. I just bought the one draw ticket because we were away. I know that doesn't make any sense? I always buy two - but this one time (not in band camp) I only bought one.

It was just one of those games and it was one of those games when they came out and basically bulldozed themselves and the ball into the back of our net after only five minutes after defender Gavin Hoyte scored after picking up a pass from Sam Togwell. And the bulldozing continued…

They knocked us about and some of the referee's decisions were bizarre. And the playing conditions were awful. Wind. Rain. Not to mention the monotonous choral selection from the home supporters. In all sincerity - I thought I was listening to a thousand cannibals drumming up a sacrifice!

So - once again – the noise and behaviour at the ground added further fears that something foul tasting is spreading through the English football leagues. FGR. Akinfenwa. Hannibal Hive.

It was our first defeat since 24 November and even though we lost - we were by far the better footballing side.

Stu Sinclair had a blinder. I know it's a bit unheard of for him not to have a great game - but his second half effort from outside the eighteen yard box would have been a contender for goal of the season if it had dropped in. And like the stalwart that he is - he soldiered on following a horrific tackle by Andy Yiadom who then saw red again. Marching orders from the referee. His only decent decision of the game.

And Lawrence? Again - not far away from a similar honour if his strike had found the back of the net.

The ugliest side in League Two came out with one intention and one intention only from the start of the game - to bully a result and indeed win ugly. And it paid off for them.

It happens. And it was probably allowed to happen because the ref made a decision to allow it to happen for fear of being eaten by the hungry home horde.

But would we have won if Rory was with us? Maybe not. Who knows? But what I do know is the result of the half time draw. The draw which I only bought one ticket for when I usually by two? Well, the bloke standing right next to me one it! It was just one of those draws. One of those queues. One of those days!

Winning every game isn't realistic. And by that - I don't mean we didn't need someone like him up front. We did. His kind of playing talent opens up other players' talents around him and we were clearly bogged down in and around their penalty area.

But it was just a grim game against a grim side followed by grim supporters who were celebrating being Conference League Champions - five months into a new season which saw them grab an ugly one-nil win against us to put them ten positions below us in the league table.

And so we left the tin stadium and I felt really sad. Not because we'd lost. I felt really sad because I'd just witnessed the terrible truth of mad minds caused by the consumption of human flesh and I was afraid it was spreading...

This result didn't gnaw away at me for any length of time. One defeat in eight games? That's impressive as far as I'm concerned. And what's also impressive is the number of Gasheads who descended on that wet and miserable place.

There were more of us than them. So you've got to love the irony of it all. They filled their tin hut with sounds of "Conference Champions" - but they couldn't outnumber us at their own ground! Then again - most home crowds struggle against our Blue Army!

Then it was time for Oxford!

7 RED HOT LOVE

OXFORD 1 V BRISTOL ROVERS 2
16TH JANUARY 2016

It was the Monday following our defeat away to Barnet that I seriously considered posting a request on all Bristol Rovers social media sites for all ginger Gasheads to stay away from the Memorial Stadium - as well as the centre of the city.

Now - as you well know - great things come in small doses so it was with amazement that I noticed the number of 'sightings' of 'Rory Gaffney' within the ground and within the vicinity of the home of Bristol Rovers FC.

Now this was extremely unusual. It obviously wasn't the striker from County Galway presenting himself to a pen and a piece of paper and it was highly unlikely there was a ginger convention taking place in the northern suburbs of Bristol. I would have known about it because I would've received an invitation.

The sightings of *Golden Hair* in the area were flooding the internet as the frenzy to see him return to his true home reached fever pitch.

It was incredible for me to witness when it began. The rise of the red had sparked forth a fervour from which the ginger was being hailed and held aloft and worshipped.

The new found reverence for those of pale and freckle even transcended where no one thought would ever be possible.

No more the cougar dating sites with members requesting tall and olive and dark. Oh no! The colour of fire was now the rage for lustful women and rampant red was now the desire.

Many women were unable to fulfil their own fantasies fuelled by the allure of auburn. Vows and bands of gold denied them the unique experience which so many now were craving - and so the alternative resulted in many high street stores reporting an increase in factor fifty sales. If they couldn't have a ginger in the flesh - then they were damned if they couldn't sniff one!

They wanted hot from the new-sparked flame of head and it was all down to the arrival and ascent of Gaffers - the man to whom ten thousand voices in song had sung, *"Oh Rory Gaffney you are the love of my life. Oh Rory Gaffney I'll let you shag my wife. Oh Rory Gaffney - I want ginger hair too!"*

Our kind were being seen everywhere and everyone wanted to see one of us. For so long we'd had to hide amid the shadows for fear of being ridiculed and scorned and sunburnt. But now those days were over with the lighting of a certain flame from the Emerald Isle.

It was on! Our time had come. It was on and if you weren't a ginger - then you wanted to be on one.

Sightings of red of hair soared in Bristol as the frenzy to see his return became an obsession with the blue and white faithful. Any ginger anywhere near the co-ordinates which pinpointed the centre of our pitch was identified as Gaffers - including a group of exchange students from Beijing who'd attempted to embrace life in the west by buying a box of L'oreal ash blonde and fucking up the mix with extra peroxide. A mistake which left them sour instead of sweet - but still very popular with amateur Gashead paparazzi wandering up Gloucester Road.

It was fever pitch! We all wanted him back and anyone with freckles became a legitimate target to be photographed and for the pic to be posted on Facebook. Threads abounded with comments like *'It's him!* to *'We've got our ginger back'* to *'Why have you posted a pic of Jimmy Krankie from last night at the Hippodrome?'*

Despite it all I knew why it was happening. It was frustrating to see because I felt the same. I wanted him back. And I don't mind saying I was desperate to see his return. But I wasn't optimistic.

From what I'd heard - Higgs wasn't interested in spending money and that information was passed on to me courtesy of a window cleaner in Kingswood. And my 'source with a sponge' knows everything. He should do because he can get away with looking in everyone's windows!

But all joking aside - it escalated quickly and it wasn't long before Gasheads from far and wide were also in Twitter typing #freerory!

This just frustrated me even more because I wanted to see his return but I had a feeling it just wasn't going to happen.

Why on earth would Shaun Derry do a deal which would see the on-form Gaffers return to the Mem - when his side would be heading to the same ground two months later?

Maybe Cambridge needed the money? Who knows? But what I do know is that for three days and nights I climbed the walls.

It was all I could think about. And more and more pictures were appearing on social media of 'Rory' entering our ground. There was even a video clip of him standing behind the Blackthorn end with an acoustic guitar singing 'All of the Stars'!

My frustration was building and building until it turned into anger and that anger continued to build and build in the minutes and hours and days which saw us move closer and closer to our next fixture which was away to Oxford United. And as the anger turned to fury - I did what any red-blooded, muscle-rippling man would do. I fixed my fearsome gaze to the match which lay ahead. And wrote a poem!

Sound keep the faith to battle new,

Hear Goodnight call to faith and true,

See ice of sky on frosty dew,

Hear blue the army March on you.

See eyes befall the quest now dear,

To more than ten and one this year,

As thousands gaze on chalice clear,

Attain with fight and feel no fear.

To Kassam comes the Rover true,

Of quarter white with heart of blue,

Hear Song like distant thunder come,

Of Irene's call - this day of Sun.

My rage and frustration was expelled through words in rhyme at the very moment I heard the news on the morning of the 14th of January. Rory Gaffney had returned to Bristol Rovers on a permanent basis. The deal had been done!

It was an incredible piece of news to hear and my reservations regarding Higgs and what he'd said prior to the Barnet match were quashed. I truly wasn't expecting the return to take place. So many rumours concerning 'this and that' - including a potential takeover which had been raging for months - had fuelled my apprehension regarding the return of the Irishman. Why buy if you're going to sell?

But it happened and there was a universal sigh of relief from supporters. He was that one piece we all believed was missing. We had all the other pieces. But before his arrival on loan - his piece was nowhere to be seen. And when he joined the squad - his piece seemed to complete the set.

It definitely felt like a time of coming together and we certainly came together to follow our team to our next League Two encounter.

We were off to a place which boasts a fine education - so we couldn't have asked for a better location to teach a lesson to a side which had beaten us one nil at home earlier in the season.

Our away clash with Oxford United took place on a Sunday and the mass of Blue Army which followed Darrell Clarke's side to the Kassam Stadium made me - and I'm sure many others - truly proud to be a Gashead!

Gasheads in North Stand, Kassam Stadium

Two and a half thousand of us descended on the ground and it was an incredible experience to be part of. Our initial ticket allocation had been for two thousand one hundred briefs. But the demand by Bristol Rovers supporters was so big - another three hundred were awarded by the Grenoble Road side.

We arrived at the ground a few hours before kick-off and I remember it was a miserable day. It really was cold - but spirits were high following the return of our favourite flame-haired son and we were confident of at least a draw following our previous week's away loss to the cannibals with drums on Camrose Avenue.

It was my first time at this ground and upon our arrival I couldn't help feeling that something was missing. It wasn't Gaffney. It wasn't a sea of blue and white. And it wasn't Helen's lucky pants.

It took me a while to realise what was nowhere to be seen. And then I saw it. Well, I didn't really see it because it isn't there. The Kassam stadium only has three sides and so it looks more like a giant blue and white dustpan.

It looks strange and it feels strange but it's quite an impressive set-up. There's a ten pin bowling alley with a bar and a place to get something to eat just across the car park from the stadium itself. Not bad at all and so we rushed into warmth of the fun factory.

The place was mobbed and there were occasional sounds in song of Irene drifting and lifting upwards from difference groups of Gasheads amid the mass of hundreds of supporters who were packed in with us - so many that the door staff had to stop other fans from entering because the venue was just rammed with blue and white and pint and chants and song.

So we were lucky to get in. A lot of poor souls had to stand outside and wait in a queue - only allowed entry when others departed the premises to head across the car park and into the stadium itself. So it was with much concern that I saw lots of our supporters outside - wearing blue and turning blue thanks to the freezing elements. At one point I thought about doing the honourable thing and leaving so that a fellow Gashead comrade could be allowed in. But then I came to my senses. Not for selfish reasons. Oh no. Not at all. It's just that my prosthetic leg isn't the Arctic design and its prone to squeaking in sub-zero temperatures. And when it does that - I find it extremely difficult to creep up on people.

So I sat down again and indulged in another bottle of orange and passion fruit J20 - because that's how I roll these days. Edgy!

And then it was time to make our way into the stadium and it really was impressive to see over two thousand of us in the ground's north stand. Two and a half thousand Gasheads at an away game. For me - that's more than impressive. That's unique! And there's definitely something that's a different kind of special in being on the road to support the Rovers.

Helen and I do our best to go to as many away matches as possible. And when we do - we tend to go with our mates Claire and Simon and we take turns with the driving.

I love these days away and we enjoy them when we can afford them. If I was rolling in cash - I'd go to every single match of the season. No problem. It's just an incredible feeling to be on the road in support of our team and the supporters I've met at away games always represent our club in the best way possible.

I've never seen a Gashead involved in any kind of fracas - either away or at home. I know I'm a newbie to the family - but I've been to to many matches already and I've never witnessed any Bristol Rovers supporter getting out of hand at a game.

Okay, I've just remembered one time and that match was the cup clash at Ashton Gate in 2013. One. I saw one Rovers supporter run onto the pitch. One. Now that says something to me. And that was reinforced when thousands of their fans invaded the pitch at the final whistle and tried to goad us into a fight. No one moved. We just stood and sang Goodnight Irene with scarves aloft and even the football commentators remarked on how impressed they were, "Those Bristol Rovers supporters are doing themselves proud!"

And I think that's maybe what it is? We're proud. We don't say, *"Proud to be a Gashead"* for nothing. It actually has worth. It means something to us. It most certainly means something to me. And I've seen this pride in so many ways when at home or away. And what I was to see at the Kassam Stadium was to typify what I mean...

The first half of the match came to an end with neither side finding the back of the net. So myself and Simon headed down and into the concourse level to get the Bovrils and Twix's. And it's what I saw and heard as we entered the concourse that will always reinforce what I've just written.

It was mobbed with Gasheads and the queues were massive. The atmosphere - despite no scoring - was one of celebration. It's almost as if being on the road in support of our team is a celebration in itself. And I suppose it is!

It was as I reached the counter to be served that it began. I did have my camera on me as I always do - but I really didn't have the opportunity to capture the following moment because it was absolutely mobbed and I could barely move - let alone carry hot drinks and chocolates and film too.

Now, in the run up to this particular game - there'd been a song which some Gasheads had started to sing at some of the matches. But you know what it's like? These new chants tend to take a bit of time to 'take off' and so it could sometimes be heard at the Memorial Stadium and at other grounds before this Oxford game - but it was by no means rapturous. Almost like a gentle wave of sound rising from whoever the tune belonged to…

I don't believe in coincidences. I haven't for a long time. Ginger had become trendy for the first time in human history - courtesy of Rory Gaffney and his boot. And it was at this time that another ginge was about to make his presence known to the Gashead faithful in a way which rocked the Kassam with a BOOM!

Ashley Belsten is a fine young example of a Bristol Rovers supporter. Tall. Athletic and red of head - Belsten personifies what it is to be a Gashead. And the song which was to rock the away concourse level on this cold Sunday afternoon was all his doing…

It began on a train last September following our away draw against Plymouth when the BRFC away days gang were having a sing off against one another. And Ashley's entry stole the show!

'When Johnny Comes Marching Home' is the tune and everyone was singing along using *"La la la la la lala lala lala lala!"*

Simple and catchy. And it was at the Kassam at half time where it really did catch on! The whole concourse level erupted and it was an incredible mass of madness in song which I will never forget. Hundreds and hundreds of Gasheads bouncing up and down – some on the shoulders of others – with lager being emptied from great height all over those who were jumping up and down in a rapturous sound of mass euphoria as "La la la la la lala lala lala lala" did its very best to blow the roof off the stadium. And we hadn't scored yet!

That's what I mean when I only see pride in celebration whenever we're at home or on the road. There's no trouble. Only an expression of being proud to follow a team which has struggled for so long in its history – to follow now in a time which now sees the dawn of success from a potential which has always been since 1883.

I had to leave them all as the mayhem continued and I'm sure I saw a ginger being thrown into the air at one point?

I'm not sure if it was Ashley? He's probably too big to be thrown about. So the fact that Gasheads were catapulting ginger midgets into the air was a clear sign that the song had become a success and the new strawberry blonde trend was truly being embraced and being welcomed in celebration.

The second half began and it was Kemar Roofe who opened the scoring for the home side just minutes after the restart. But Matty Taylor netted a great header six minutes later following a stunning run down the right by Danny Leadbitter.

Bristol Rovers supporters celebrate Ellis Harrison penalty

Jermaine Easter and Ellis Harrison replaced Taylor and Gaffney and it was this duo who clinched the winner with just two minutes of time remaining.

Easter was brought down in the box and Ellis did what he does from the penalty spot. And that was that!

Two and a half thousand Gasheads went nuts in the north stand as Harrison and his teammates raced towards the frenzy of blue and white which had hit the road from Bristol earlier that day. That day which was -for me - the perfect away day.

We departed the Kassam sitting fourth in League Two on forty six points and there's no better feeling than driving away from an away clash with three points in the bag.

But as we sat in the car listening to the results coming in from the other matches – the news broke regarding our game's penalty scorer joining Hartlepool for a month on loan. Ellis Harrison…

Up next was our Memorial match against the side we'd played and drawn against in September and from which the *"La la la la"* song was born. Plymouth…

8 THE REASON

I remember looking into her eyes and seeing the life of her drain away. And I know it was from that point in my own life that something became no more...

I was sixteen years old and I was walking home from rugby practice when it happened. And what was to happen was an awful phenomenon which had begun to spread across the country.

I grew up in Southern Africa. Zimbabwe and South Africa. And my formative years were spent in a time in history in those two places where extreme violence was commonplace and simply accepted as normal.

The fall of Apartheid was imminent. It was clear for all to see. And there were many who refused to accept the inevitable. Family murder-suicides began making news headlines and they continued to do so for many years.

I was sixteen and I was walking home from training at school when I passed a large house and heard several loud bangs coming from the garage next to the house and the top of the long driveway. And then I heard the screaming - a sound which stopped me from moving any further.

A young girl about my age emerged from the garage and she was still screaming as she ran towards me - arms open as she pleaded for me to, *"Help them! Help them!"* And then she ran away.

I think I watched her for a few seconds and then turned my attention to the darkened entrance to the garage from where the girl had appeared. I couldn't see anything and all had gone quiet. So I began walking up the driveway towards the dark of the entrance to see if I could find out what had happened…

I put my school bag down onto the grass near the entrance to the garage before walking inside. And because I'd just entered the dark place from outside in the bright sunlight - I struggled to see what was inside as I stepped in.

My eyes adjusted to the dimness and I saw a car over to the right hand side of the garage. The four doors were open and so was the boot - with what looked like grocery shopping spilled across the concrete floor.

Peering towards the car - I could see someone sitting in the back seat and so I walked over and looked in through the open door. A boy who looked a few years younger than me was sitting upright with his head tilted to the right and resting on his shoulder. And then I saw the hole just above his left ear as the blood trickled down into his neck. And I just knew he was gone.

I didn't panic. I didn't run. I just took a step back and began looking around because now I could see more clearly within the dimness of the garage. And then I saw the man.

The man was laying on his back and he was still. He too had a wound in his head and there was an automatic firearm on the ground next to him. And I remember just not knowing what to do or say.

Everything began to feel hazy within the garage and then I could feel my legs getting heavy as I struggled to move. And that's when I saw her...

The woman was on her hands and knees and she was on the floor right in front of me. She staring straight at me and she was trying to tell me something. Her mouth was moving but no sound came. And as I slowly knelt down to try and hear what she was trying to tell me - I saw three holes in her chest from which her life was spilling onto the concrete floor.

I don't know how long I knelt before her as she spoke her silent words to me. But all the time I kept her gaze. And as I kept her gaze - I saw the life slowly drift away from her eyes.

What could have been seconds or minutes later - I managed to get a grip of myself and ran outside and started calling for help. I ran into a neighbouring house and told them to phone the police. They did.

I didn't know what else to do. So I just sat on the grassy verge opposite the house where the woman was in the garage and I waited.

The police and the ambulances arrived and they tried their best to keep her alive. I could see them. But they stopped after a while and covered her with a sheet before taking her and her son and husband away in the ambulance.

I was sixteen when I witnessed the immediate aftermath of a family murder-suicide. No counselling was offered and I took a day off school the following day. I seemed fine.

My life continued and I finished school and found a job as a trainee civil engineering draftsman. But then I volunteered to do my national service and was allowed to choose my posting.

I chose the military police. I wanted a career as a military lawyer. I was told that for that to happen - I'd first have to serve eighteen months fighting in the bush alongside combat units in South West Africa and Angola. I agreed. I'd just turned twenty.

Two weeks before I was due to begin my basic training - I was involved in a terrible car crash in the middle of nowhere. I lost control of the car and hit a crash barrier which impaled the car and crushed my right foot so badly that it came off in the car.

I remember the impact but only vaguely. I then regained consciousness as I lay in a field next to the car wreck. I remember a strange tingly sensation on the end of my right leg. I couldn't sit up. It hurt. So I lifted my leg to take a look and all I saw was bone and skin where my foot used to be.

I wasn't in any pain. Shock must have set in. But I was scared to lower my leg. I didn't want anything to stick into the wound and hurt me. So I just kept my leg raised as high as I could. But I knew I was in trouble. I was in the middle of nowhere on an empty stretch of road in the African bush. So I started to realise that I was going to bleed to death. And then I remembered the woman in the garage as I looked up at the blue sky and watched the white clouds pass overhead.

It was if by seeing her life disappear from her eyes - I knew she must have been going somewhere. And that helped me to find peace in knowing that there was somewhere to go.

At that point there was an overwhelming calmness which seemed to hold me. It was beautiful in its serenity and helped me to find comfort in what was happening - even though I felt sad about not seeing my family again.

And then I heard a voice within me say, *"John. You have to keep your leg up. You have to do this!"*

The voice was firm and it sounded more like an order than a request.

I was found by a unit of army guys who were doing their own basic training. They belonged to the signals core and immediately radioed for help.

I found out later that they said it was the most bizarre thing they'd ever seen. I was unconscious when they found me - but my leg was up in the air. And that's what saved my life.

I recovered and learned how to walk again with a prosthetic leg. And my life continued.

My return to the United Kingdom happened in 1993 and it was the following year that I got a lucky break and started working in broadcasting as a runner for different productions.

I was determined to do the best I could and I worked hard to learn as much as I could whenever I could. So I worked my way up from runner to researcher in politics and current affairs to newsroom journalist and reporter to assistant producer in sport.

Further promotions to producer and director in football programming were to come at a time when I also fell in love and got married. I had a lovely wife and home and career and I had many, many friends and colleagues. I had it all. Including alcoholism.

I'm very fortunate. The illness never wrecked my career and I still maintain a good relationship with former colleagues in Glasgow - colleagues who I still miss. I just ended up taking more and more time off work because of the addiction. And then they offered me a healthy redundancy package which I accepted. They did their best to help me. And for that I will always be grateful.

My wife and friends tried their best too. But they were up against something they didn't understand. And neither did I.

My marriage ended and I had to move away from Glasgow. I ended up in Ipswich in 2007. Family were there and they did their best too. But the illness had me by this point and I ended up living in a homeless hostel where all I could think about was my next drink. It was my rock bottom.

The intervention came on the morning of the 7th of June 2010. I sat alone – a man broken in a small, stinking room surrounded by empty bottles. I was unrecognisable.

Everything and everyone had gone. I'd been relegated as a person.

And then my phone rang. It was the crisis team and they asked me if I was ready to change. I said yes. And for the first time in six years I meant it.

They said to wait where I was. So I just sat on the edge of the dirty bed and as I looked down towards the floor - I saw a bottle which was half full with vodka. And it was then that the same voice within me - the voice from the car crash - said, *"No more for you! You have suffered enough!"*

Staff from the Drug and Alcohol Crisis team arrived about half an hour later and took me away. I was ready within myself to begin my recovery. I'd been knocked down before. I was ready to fight my way back again. And when we left the stinking room - the bottle was still half full and I haven't touched a drop since...

I was sent to residential rehab in Weston Super Mare and it was in this incredible place that I was helped to find the real me.

I walked through the doors with only a small bag of personal belongings and an emptiness within myself. And five months later I walked away with a few more bags - but filled with a new hope for me in a new life. And Bristol was my destination.

I met Helen eighteen months later and she is now my love. Helen and her girls and her mum. I also have a new and better relationship with my own family too.

You see - that day in May 2014 was a day which had a profound effect on me. Even though I hadn't fallen in love with our club at that point - I saw the hurt and tears and anger that relegation had brought to those who I knew and loved - those who were standing next to me in the north terrace.

So I made a decision. I knew - as I stood on the steps of the Blackthorn End - what it meant to be sent down. I'd felt my own hurt and tears and anger in my own life when I was relegated as a person. And that's when a deep connection was made between myself and our club. It was that simple and yet if felt so very powerful. And I know that connection will always remain because my past experiences will always remain within me.

So I decided to follow our club and in my own small way - be part of the following which followed our gaffer and our lads down there and back again. And it is and always will be one of the best decisions I've ever made!

I don't profess to know the reasons why we do the things we do and why we step towards what we're drawn to through hurt. But it does seem that loss can bring us closer to passions and that passions can also hold us close when we're hurt.

Helen's own love for the Rovers was born at the moment she saw Ollie fall to his knees at the end of the 1988/1989 season when we reached the third division play-off final for the first time but failed to win promotion - losing by a single goal to Port Vale. She saw him fall to his knees in tears and that was when something deep within her connected to our club and that 'something' commanded that she should follow. So she did. And she always will.

These loves for Bristol Rovers also hold us close when we feel as if we can't go on. Carole - Helen's mum - has been a Gashead for longer than her daughter and it was our club which gave her a reason to live through the grief of losing her son Antony in 1991. He was only nineteen when he suddenly collapsed and died through heart failure.

Carole was broken. But every week for ninety minutes she found brief respite from her grief when the Gas were playing. For ninety minutes at Twerton - she was just like everyone else at the ground. She was a Bristol Rovers supporter and her love for our club was one of the few reasons which gave her some kind of strength to face each new day for many, many days.

Carole wrote to Geoff Twentyman and thanked him and his fellow team mates for helping her to find some kind of solace in her life - even if it was only between the whistle blows which start and end a match.

Life. Football isn't just a game. You hear it all the time from supporters all over the world. Football is a way of life.

That means the game is just as much a part of your life as it is your experiences in life which draw you towards standing on the terraces on a Saturday afternoon. And those life experiences which draw you to the terraces are also ones filled with happiness and joy.

It's not just about the hurt. But for me - the connection made with the game through hurt is a connection which can also deliver an equal but opposite experience. One of elation. And that was to prove true for me personally on the 7th of May 2016. I'm sure it was for you too!

9 PSYCHIC KNEECAPS

BRISTOL ROVERS 1 V PLYMOUTH 1
23RD JANUARY 2016

It was a west country derby as league leaders Plymouth visited the Memorial Stadium and I knew this was my chance to impress local media with a match report like no other...

I'd been away from football journalism for quite a while - but I just knew I had it in me to deliver something special. This is what I wrote and sent to local broadcasters...

'You know it's coming. You can feel it coming. But you just don't know when it's coming.

And you only know it's coming because your knees are telling you it's coming and it's been like this since you awakened to being a Gashead at Dover last season.

You're not sure how it happens? But it does happen and it's as if you've developed psychic patellas since you donned the blue and white quarters with pride and passion and also started introducing the word *'mind'* at the end of every sentence. Proper like…

Your kneecaps began heightening around the 69th minute of the match and this number leaves you slightly confused - because it's unheard of in the beautiful game for both sets of supporters to be revelling in ecstasy at the same time - unless Arsenal are at home to Spurs and word of Chelsea getting thumped alerts thousands of app phones in the stadium!

So your knees are banging as distant memories of that particular kind of indulgence dematerialise in your mind - to be replaced by the sounds of booing as the Blackthorn End once again extends its justified discontent at the bungling buffoon in black who's behaving in a way which suggests a nine and sixty is an experience which has been denied him - even though he's surely faced an arsehole on many occasions because referees have to be clean shaven to officiate a game.

So it's coming. You know it's coming and your knees are telling you it's coming. And as you're writing these words you become uncomfortably aware that you're using words like 'coming' and 'knee trembler' and now you're hoping you don't get banned from media organisaitons in the south west for pushing the boundaries of public decency.

But you're sure your gratuitous innuendo will be laughed at and not taken seriously - a bit like 'them down the road' and their delusion concerning a 'gap'!

And then it happens. It's Billy Bodin in the 79th minute and his close range header sets off a rapture in sound - directed towards the twilight sky from nine thousand hearts of blue and a flailing of punching fists amid a frenzy of elation and relief. And it's a scene which would have seen your Viking forefathers proud as a beserker of sound silences a thousand pilgrims who've only managed a miserable murmur since the arsehole blew his whistle seventy nine match minutes earlier.

You can't describe the frenzy. You don't have to for those who were there. But it's as if time and space stops and you're devoid of all the world - with the exception of sharing a primal scream with thousands of others as you grab your mate who grabs you back as you both jump up and down in the most delicious madness you'll ever know - whilst catching a glimpse of the player who scored being smothered by other players because his performance was on fire and now they're trying to put him out.

Irene then rises and if the pilgrims weren't silenced before - then they sure as hell are now. No one survives that - and it's as her rallying call from history, passion and fight echoes into the night sky that you feel something else coming from another psychic part of your anatomy.

This time it's not your knees. This time it's your stomach. And this time it feels as if invisible hands have reached inside you to perform some kind of spiritual surgery - as the fingers unseen pull and tug and stretch in the same way you pull and tug and stretch a balloon before you blow it up - as the fear is twisting you inside out because ten minutes remain and six hundred seconds is a long, long time to hold on to clinch a home victory to remember.

And as your stomach is twisting - you notice your arse cheeks are trembling. And that's a first!

They equalize. You're disappointed - not gutted. - because it's a point against a team on form and they're not sitting top of the table for nothing but the referee is awful and he has words with gaffers on several occasions for reasons which are beyond all reasonable comprehension.

Rory Gaffney supporters supporting Bristol Rovers v Plymouth

And then you realise he probably just wants an excuse to talk to your fiery headed forward because he's probably also fallen in love with the Irish striker - just like the many ginger wig wearing Gasheads dotted all over the memorial in a sign that the ginger revolution has started.

So it finished a one-one draw at the Memorial Stadium and the result sees Darrell Clarke's men remain in fourth place - four points behind automatic promotion places and it's a match weekend which sees Plymouth toppled from top spot by Northampton.'

I'm still waiting to hear from the media organisations as to whether or not they're interested in taking me on?

Accrington Stanley 1 v 0 Bristol Rovers

30th January 2016

The Gas were on the road again and we had a history with opposition in as much they were our jinx.

Accrington had visited the Mem in September and walked away with the three points after Billy Kee's overhead kick and the match finished 0-1 to the visitors.

Penultimate day in January and Darrell Clarke's men suffer the same result on the road and Rovers remain in fourth position - just four points away from the automatic promotion positions.

10 SQUIDGY TRUTH

The rumours had been alive for months. But the universal feeling amongst Gasheads was that although it would be incredible to have a new owner with money to invest in the club - the idea was just too good to be true!

"Nothing like that ever happens for us," was the general viewpoint and yet the speculation continued.

But you know what they say about smoke - it's great for curing haddock and if you get it just right - the fish lasts quite a long time and it tastes delicious.

But it did seem as if there was a fire somewhere and lots of supporters were stating so online - that they'd heard from a mate who works in the shop down the road, next to the off license opposite the chippy which sells smoked fish where an American customer on holiday told him that a Canadian financier knew a London investor who was pulling together a consortium which was interested in funding another consortium to fund an offer to Nick Higgs - who loves smoked Haddock. And that was coming from the Kingswood window cleaner.

So there had to be some truth in it? And I found out there was some truth in it. Higgs likes a fish supper! Don't we all!

It had been going on for so long that I completely lost interest in it all - especially since a lot of the rumour mongers were also scaremongers in suggesting that new owners would change everything the club held dear - including our strip colours, badge, mascot, Captain Gas, anthems, the woman who sells the fifty-fifty draw tickets at the north stand turnstiles and our chicken tikka pie. And those are to name but a few.

It was just ridiculous. Who the hell would want to get rid of the chicken tikka pie if they bought the club? It's the perfect meal for losing weight. It's rammed with calories - yet helps you to shift pounds and lightens the readings on your electronic scales. You eat it. It fills you up. And then you shit yourself thin. All three desires taken care of in one foul experience wrapped in pastry. It's genius.

However, in all seriousness, something was rumbling. You could feel it rumbling. To many people were talking about rumbling for something not to be rumbling. And I'm not talking about the after effects of that pie. And there was something in the air and it had nothing to do with the consequences of that pasty either.

And so I wrote something in early February. It was Saturday the 6th of February and I was bored. I was bored because our match against the Wombles at home had been cancelled due to rain which saw a flood of biblical proportions take place at the Mem. It was bad. But not as bad as the swarm of locusts that fell on Yeovil. Not much we could've done with our punishment from above. The best we could have done was go for a swim. But I heard that walking through Yeovil town centre that night was like walking through Bangkok with all the locals munching on deep fried crunchy things.

You've got to hand it to them. Come to think of it - maybe not. Don't hand anything to them. It just gets them confused and upset when they see five fingers on a hand.

So where was I? Oh yeah – writing in bed. I usually write about Saturday's match at night when I'm tucked up just before I go to sleep. It's just something I do. I also do it if I need to find calmness after I've seen something which unsettles me.

I had to write a lot on the night of new arrival Rory Fallon's Haka. It scared the shit into me when I first saw it. I thought the poor bloke was reacting to those pies – because if he had - it would have scared the shit out of him.

But the worst was the night of the first appearance of a certain 'Gashead X-Factor Wannabe' who decided he was going to sing to the camera on his phone.

It wouldn't have bothered me to be honest - but what left me feeling extremely vulnerable and confused was the fact that he didn't just sing to his phone - he recorded it and posted it onto the BRFC Facebook page for all to see. And hear!

His face was so close to the screen - he looked like the smiling baby sun from Teletubbies. With a goatee!

Now we have a cat and his name is Bob. We rescued him because he wasn't being looked after properly. He's pure white, deaf, a bit retarded and his back legs don't work. So he doesn't walk - he wobbles and he bumps into things and screams at the sky quite a lot. So he fits in quite well in our house.

The reason I'm mentioning Bob is because he saw and didn't hear the aforementioned songster and I'm convinced I saw a little glint of something spark approval in his eyes. And that's worrying. It's a bit like receiving a nod of approval from Sloth from *The Goonies*.

The songster chose that famous ditty from the seventies by Boney M, *"Brown girl in the Ring"* and he featured words to do with our defender - Lee Brown - and ended with the line, *"Bum, bum, bum!"* instead of *"Tra-la-la!"*

The horror doesn't just end with that one. There were more to come. And they're still coming. And the funny thing is - I think he's now gaining a following!

But reactions were mixed following his debut on screen video. Many fans took it for what it was - a bit of fun. Although I'm sure many more screamed and ran and dived behind the sofa!

But others responded with outrage - with a few supporters calling him a 'type' of pervert.

Now I thought this was a bit harsh because being rubbish at singing and being in a music video hardly makes a person a pervert. If it did - then half the faces sitting at the Grammy's would be on some kind of list.

To be honest - I almost fell off my chair laughing out loud when I first saw one of those 'pervert' comments. It was just so ridiculous! Most of the contestants on the X-Factor can't sing and there's hardly a van waiting to take them to HMP Strangeways if they don't appear on the Christmas number one single.

No likey? No watchy!

There's a great quote by the eminent Swiss psychiatrist, Carl Jung *""Everything that irritates us about others can lead us to an understanding of ourselves."*

But these reactions have now softened and I genuinely think he'll be making his television debut at some point in the near future.

Hats off to you mate. I haven't named you for legal reasons. But you know who you are and we definitely know who you are! Long may your reign continue. If we can't indulge in a bit of amusing mayhem and madness from time to time - what's the point in it all hey?

So where was I? Oh, yeah - the alleged takeover by some kind of consortium.

So I was lying in bed on the night of the Memorial flood and I began writing in reaction to some of the fears which supporters had been posting online. In all seriousness – they were all legitimate apprehensions. Takeovers mean change and change can leave people feeling fearful. So this is what I wrote on the 6th of February 2016:

'We've got our Rovers back' means something very different to me because I'm new to being a Gashead. I only witnessed the tail-end of the fall into the non-league abyss.

I say this amid continued speculation regarding an imminent takeover which will involve either Americans, Londoners or Middle Eastern Royalty - a speculation which, within some quarters - seems to connect the dismissal of what we've found again with the spectre of financiers who remain unseen, yet known amongst those who are unlikely to know.

But all joking aside - if there is a consortium within the periphery of the Memorial shadows - would it really be in its best interests to alienate supporters by ravaging what we've only recently found again?

We know it happens and we know it has happened elsewhere. But does that mean the same is a certainty if it takes place on our own turf? My own feeling in that one is, *"No!"*

If I had £100 million and I was intent on buying BRFC - it would be to make money through success. It would be an investment. And a massive part of that cash injection into the business would be to take the club forward so that it would make more money amid more achievements on the pitch. And that would require substantial investment into playing staff and an arena which would complement the vision of a new ethos. Success.

A massive part of that envisaged success is, without doubt, the supporters. A football club isn't a football club without supporters. And the Blue Army is a following like no other.

Any potential investor worth their weight will have already identified this and our following of DC and his squad into the Conference - where we broke attendance records for fun - is testament to the true and real potential which exists within our club. And this potential lays within the history and traditions held close by supporters.

So why change this aspect of the club? Why dismiss tradition and history - when it could spark an exodus of fans who have money in their pockets? That doesn't make sense to me.

Fair enough - the Bluebirds saw red in 2012 following their own takeover by a Malaysian businessman. But their supporters made sure Mr Tan ended up singing the blues and their traditional colour was restored last year.

So don't be put off by a potential investor potentially changing our history just because it happened elsewhere - albeit briefly. That would be an acknowledgement that we'd just accept changes which are unacceptable. And that will never happen. We're Gasheads. We're faithful and true.

And heaven help anyone who tries to mess with our traditions which span generations.

I just can't see it happening. The wise move would be to invest in every aspect of or club - including our traditions because there's also a lot of money to be made on that front too. Merchandise sales is a massive part in any football club's revenue. And it's the supporters who fill that particular coffer. So why upset supporters and deny yourself an income? It doesn't make sense and I truly believe it's not worth worrying about.

But there would be changes. And maybe not all for the good.

I love the Mem. I love the Mem because it was in the Blackthorn End that I fell in love with our club. And I know a part of me will be ripped apart the day we move into 'Plan B'. But for me - for survival to take place - change has to happen.

That change has to happen to ensure some kind of planned and measured success to take place - success which will comfortably steer us well clear of ever allowing the events of 3rd of May 2014 from happening again.

Our history deserves it. But that means change and change can be scary. But always remember it can never be as scary as Big Blissett on the receiving end of a pass. Although he's having a great time now with Torquay United!

If this imminent takeover - which is universally known about within the window cleaning fraternity of Kingswood ᵣₛ ᵤrue, then it leaves me naturally apprehensive but excited too.

My apprehension is simply down to entering the unknown. But my excitement is based purely on the possibilities of where substantial investment could take our history. And can you imagine the possibilities. I can. And they outweigh any apprehensions.'

11 NOT SAVED BY THE BELL

PORTSMOUTH 3 V BRISTOL ROVERS 1
13TH FEBRUARY 2016

I stopped watching our lads and actually focussed on watching the home side in the second half.

For most of the first half - I didn't know where to look. And there were two reasons for that.

The first and foremost reason for me looking everywhere except the pitch was because it was extremely difficult to watch what was happening on the pitch - or what wasn't happening.

There's a saying which Helen uses from time to time, "They tore us a new arsehole!" And that was bang-on for what happened to us at Fratton Park on that day in February.

We were standing just behind the goals in the Milton End and about three rows from the front. And I did notice I was standing in an odd way during the opening forty five minutes. A bit like a giraffe having a drink. And that was probably courtesy of what I was seeing because what I was seeing was tearing me a new arsehole.

So I found it difficult to watch. And it was difficult to not watch too. So I found myself watching the match and then looking across to my left and then right and then over to the Fratton End before returning once again to what wasn't supposed to be happening on the pitch.

I think I even looked behind me a few times too. Fuck knows why? It's not as if I was going to find any words of reassurance because when I looked back - everyone else was looking to their right and left as I'd just been doing and it's highly likely they were also looking for the same thing I was trying to find. So I ended up with a sore arsehole and a sore neck.

Amid my search for some kind of saviour - I was also doing my best to find the cow. But I did give up on that one and put it down to some kind of stress-induced auditory phenomenon.

The home side ran riot and goals by Gareth Evans and Michael Smith put Pompey in a sound 2-0 lead at half time.

Their third came in the 77th minute from Marc McNulty and that was the proverbial nail in the proverbial coffin.

Browner took a lot of stick after the game despite scoring a stunning late free kick. Bet he isn't taking any stick now as I write these words which you're reading!

So I'd been watching the home side for most of the second half and I really don't mind saying that. They were impressive to watch and we just hadn't shown up.

My peering to left and right and straight ahead continued for most of the game. I didn't really want to be there. But I'd never leave.

It's that awful feeling you have when you just want to call it a day and walk away - but you can't. You won't and you don't. You just want to stay amid some kind of hope that something incredible is going to happen and it's going to change everything and there's going to be an incredible fightback and *Fear the Beard* is going to start it all off with another blinder like the strike at Exeter and then that's going to inspire the lads and Gaffers is going to take the game by the fucking scruff of the neck and deliver his first hat trick to see sheer bedlam ensue in the Milton End as three thousand Gasheads erupt into joyous rapture as Irene reaches the Heavens!

But it doesn't and all you can think about is, *"Where is that cow?"*

The result at Fratton saw us drop out of the play-off places and into eighth position on forty seven points in League Two.

But I'd like to finish this chapter with something strange that happened. As I was looking around during the match - there was a man who got my attention. I was drawn to look him. He resembled my ex-father in law. He had silver hair and he had a nice smiley face. There was just something about him and he was standing to my left - just a few seats away.

I was to see him six days later as he sat beside two Jordanian men at a press conference at the Memorial Stadium.

12 POTENTIAL

I was driving to Bath when I heard the news on the morning of the 19th of February 2016. And it was the kind of news which inspires you to start looking for a safe place to pull over and park - because you know you're going to be on your phone for a while.

News was filtering in and onto social media sites regarding a press conference which had been announced for the Memorial Stadium. And it was there that the following statement was announced:

'League Two football club Bristol Rovers has been acquired by the eminent Jordanian Al Qadi family, it was announced today. As part of the deal Mr Wael Al Qadi will become President of the club.

Mr Al Qadi is a lifelong fan of English Football and a member of the executive board of the Jordan Football Association. The former Chairman of Swansea City, Steve Hamer, who has played a key role in the deal, will become the football club's new Chairman, replacing Nick Higgs who will step down.

Mr Al Qadi, aged 46, and a father of four, was educated at Westminster School and Boston University commented:

"I've been a passionate football fan all of my life and I'm excited to become involved with Bristol Rovers, which has such an amazing heritage and loyal fan base.

We really see the potential of this great club. Bristol Rovers has always been known as a family club and it is my family's wish to maintain that tradition, through our own involvement and commitment."

It was done!

Months and months of rumour and speculation had reached a conclusion with the announcement that we were now under new ownership and the man and his family who were now at the helm had seen our potential and decided it was a potential worth investing in!

I remember sitting in my car in a lay-by just a few hundred yards from Twerton Park when a wave of emotion hit me as huge sigh of relief came from within.

Someone so very important had seen what we knew we had. Someone of influence had seen our potential - born from our history and our passion and our traditions and our fight. And this someone was also a football fan!

Social media just erupted and it wasn't long before I started to see images from the press conference being posted on the internet.

One image showed three men sitting at the top table of the press conference and they answered questions from journalists. The man in the middle was Wael Al-Qadi -the new President of Bristol Rovers. The man to his left was his brother - Sam Al-Qadi. And the man to Wael's right was the same man with the silver hair and smiling face who I'd seen standing behind the goals at Fratton Park six days earlier - former Swansea City Chairman, Steve Hamer.

I enjoyed a wee laugh to myself. Despite the previous week's scoreline - they still went ahead with acquiring our club. Just goes to show that potential isn't just about results!

It was an incredible day following the incredible news. And that night - as I also sat and looked ahead to the match the next day against Morecambe - I wrote this:

'I'm sitting at my edit suite as I'm writing this and I'm feeling a wee bit emotional.

The question was put to our new club president, wealthy Jordanian businessman Mr Wael Al-Qadi, *"Why Bristol Rovers?"* And his answer highlighted our 'potential' which included the thousands of our supporters who descended on Wembley last May.

Gasheads. Even eminent Jordanian businessmen are impressed by who and what we are and what we are is quite simple - we're faithful and true.

We sing those words from the terraces, whether we're at home or on the road - and those words resonate a truth which is and always will be true.

I know it's only day one. But he does seem like a genuine and down to earth bloke and I think that's why I'm feeling a wee bit weepy. And I don't mind saying that because I always have been and always will be proud to be referred to as 'Ragbag' or 'Tinpot' by those who haven't got it in them to 'stay 'til the end'. And that's how I truly feel.

We haven't really had much when it comes to money. But we've always had heart and we've always had fight. Then, along came our gaffer and along with his squad - we found unity again when we all fought our way out of the Football Conference. And for me - that's priceless.

I don't have children. So I'll never have the chance to take a daughter or son to watch the Gas. But if I did have an opportunity to take a wee one along to one of our home games in our new stadium in the future - I'd tell them the story of how it all began for me. I'd tell them how I fell in love with the best supporters the football world has ever seen - because they had nothing and gave everything. And that spirit was financially affirmed on the 19th of February 2016.

It seems we now have money. And it also seems we now have a man at the helm who also sees what we've seen within each other since 1883. And that makes me smile.

A smile for me. A smile for him. A smile for our club. A smile for our squad. A smile for our manager. And a smile for our former chairman in taking the honourable step aside - as a true fan - to allow our history and traditions to move forward into a new and exciting era.

I've decided to take 'Ragbag' and 'Tinpot' with me into our new era because it was within those names that resistance in courage was forged.

And if by fate, in many years to come, I find myself wearing the blue and white quarters in one of the world's finest footballing arenas - to watch our team take on whoever - it'll be with immense pride that I answer to 'Ragbag' or 'Tinpot' because those embrace the defiance which is the essence of faithful and true - both embodied within the Gasheads of Bristol Rovers Football Club.'

13 IN AND OUT

BRISTOL ROVERS 2 V MORCAMBE 1
20TH FEBRUARY 2016

He gave us a wave!

It wasn't a complete surprise to be honest. Our new President and our new chairman were seen wandering around in the Blackthorn End as they introduced themselves to supporters before our home match with Morecambe - just hours after the announcement that they were now at the helm.

And it was from this helm that we were informed that *'evolution not revolution'* would take place over the days and weeks and months and years to come.

Success was now the objective for the club - successes achieved by implementing a new infrastructure which would provide the platform from which the successes could be attained. A realistic vision for real targets by men who have a true passion for the game.

Claire and Helen with Wael Al-Qadi

Wael Al-Qadi appeared all over social media sites and that was probably courtesy of so many selfies taken with him before the Morecambe game actually kicked-off. Profile pictures were changing all over the south west of England and as supporters to everyone on their friends list that they'd met the man from Jordan who'd made the investment into the potential they'd lived and breathed all of their lives.

For so long I'd been hearing supporters who'd followed the club for years - some of whom were born into the blue and white quarters - say that investment into Bristol Rovers would never happen. It never had and it was unlikely that it ever would.

For so long the label of being the alleged 'poor relation' to another club in the city had been worn. It was just accepted that it would always be that way. A club struggling to simply get by and it's testimony to the club's resilience that it did indeed get by.

And I'm sure that most would agree that Rovers stumbling forward was largely down to the supporters who never gave up and always stood by their club. Our club. Your club.

Testament to these words is the truth of thousands and thousands of Gasheads who stood by Darrell Clarke and his squad when they were sent down. But when that happened - they were never alone.

Our away support attendances broke non-league records during our campaign to return to where we belong - a fact which is witness to a unique passion.

A massive part of the potential of the club is the supporters. And now the man who saw that potential was mixing with ordinary folk in a place which they hold dear – a place where so many express their passion and love for the club. The Memorial Stadium.

He bought the club and the following day he introduced himself to the supporters on the terraces. Shaking hands and joining supporters for photographs. Not just the club's new President. Not just the representative of the family which had bought Bristol Rovers. It became very clear that he'd become a fan overnight as he casually said hello to hundreds of the blue and white faithful on the steps of the stands.

He was introducing himself and his family to the potential which they'd just invested in. Gasheads. And he was welcomed as one of our own.

Wael and his family walked onto the pitch before kick-off and they received a welcome in rapture and amid the applause rose the song we always sing. It simply had to be done and we wanted it that way. The waiting was over. The wait had been for so very long.

Her time began a long time ago. 1883. She just had to let him know she approved. And it was then that Irene rose in song from all over the ground - to gently fall on the Al Qadi family as they waved and smiled and laughed. Her blessing was complete.

The it was time to get down to business. Bristol Rovers at home to Morecambe…

Both sides last faced each other at the Globe Arena at the start of October in a game which saw seven goals - with both sides scoring two penalties in the final ten minutes of the game. And it was Clarke's men who returned to Bristol as 4-3 victors.

But that was then and now it was about clinching a result to get us back into a play-off position.

We were hopeful it could be achieved considering our recent run of home results - with four wins and a draw from our previous five clashes at the Mem.

The last time we'd been beaten at home was late November. And three points would be the prefect anointing for our new owner watching down from the director's box.

The game started and twelve minutes later it was Tom Parkes who got handy in the box and it was Jamie Devitt who scored from the spot.

So we were down a goal and that's when something a bit unusual happened...

Beth, Helen's daughter, had joined us for the game and it was her first time back at the Mem for four years. She's a massive football fan and a Gashead - but college and then work meant she hadn't had a lot of spare time. But with the previous day's events - she wanted to be part of the Memorial welcome for the Al Qadi family. So she joined our own regular group of misfits in the Blackthorn End.

It was just after Devitt scored from the penalty spot that Beth turned to Helen and said, *"Don't worry. We're going to win. We'll equalise in the 68th minute and our winning goal will happen shortly afterwards!"*

Now I didn't hear this. I was either trying to film some fans shots or still trying to figure out if there really was a cow at Fratton? But other people within our group had heard her prediction too. But all eyes once again returned to the match.

So the game continued and it was fair to say there was a lot of gazing being directed towards the directors box. And then someone started singing, "Wael Wael give us a wave. Wael give us a wave!"

And he did. Wael waved down towards the thousands of supporters in the north stand and a huge cheer went up from the crowd who then started to sing, "Wael is a Gashead! Wael is a Gashead! Lalalala! Lalalala!"

So into the second half and it was the Morecambe keeper - Barry Roche - who couldn't handle a Danny Leadbitter cross and that gave our Irishman the perfect opportunity from twelve yards out to deliver the equaliser we'd all been waiting for and the whole place erupted.

Amid the celebrations - I looked up towards the main stand and saw that Wael and his family were celebrating just like us. And I think I knew then that our potential had caught the eye of the right man for the job!

It was Rory Gaffney's first goal since his return to the club on a permanent basis and his volley hit the back of the net in the 68th minute!!

Everyone turned around and looked at Beth and it's fair to say they looked a bit puzzled. But not as puzzled as ten minutes later when substitute Bodin's close-range header clinched the winner!

It was a great day and it was the perfect result to welcome the Al-Qadi family to Bristol Rovers with the win seeing us jump back up into the play-off positions - sitting sixth on fifty points and five points adrift of the top three.

But the match was the last we saw of a certain player for the remainder of our promotion-winning season…

He signed for Rovers from Salisbury in June 2014 and the first time Helen and I saw him play was during a pre-season friendly against Cheltenham before the start of our non-league campaign. And what we saw was to leave us looking forward to seeing a lot more.

He just didn't stop running. He was everywhere and anywhere and it was very clear that this midfielder had an awareness and foresight which he used to offer passes and crosses in a way which seemed to suggest he was seeing the play before it had even happened.

Combine all of this with a 'look' which wouldn't have been out of place on a pirate ship and it didn't take long for him to become a much-loved favourite with the Gasheads.

Do you remember Kenilworth Road last August? The 94th minute? A great twist and turn by Taylor who then delivered a stunning ball over the heads of two defenders which was beautifully controlled by this player and he put it past the keeper of his old club to see Rovers walk away with the three points.

How about away to Exeter last November? Bodin laid the ball off for this player just outside the eighteen yard box and he delivered a beautiful strike to bury the ball in the top left hand corner of the net.

He's also generous off the pitch with his efforts and he's regularly seen visiting supporters in hospital and does so much for the good image of our club. And I don't think he does it because he's asked to do it. I know he does it because he wants to do it.

That's testament to the kind of person he is and it's a real pity he wasn't part of the playing squad which clinched our second successive promotion on the 7th of May.

Injury saw him unable to continue playing after the Morecambe game following thirty matches played this season. And it was almost exactly a year ago that he was unable to continue through to our Wembley final following 27 appearances during our Conference campaign.

His name is Stuart Sinclair and he's affectionately known as 'Fear the Beard'. These words are for you. You deserve them and I'm looking forward to seeing you back in action again in League One.

So we all walked away from the Memorial Stadium feeling very happy. It had nothing to do with our 2-1 win over Morecambe. We were very happy because we were about to bundle Beth into the car and drive her to get a lottery ticket so that we could live out our days sunning ourselves on our own private island whilst sipping chilled cocktails and listening to the Gas on the radio! And I also had an idea for a new business for our family?

14 DELICIOUS DICHOTOMY

24TH FEBRUARY 2016

I know it happened at Dover last season. I know for sure it happened near those white cliffs and what it was that happened was to leave me twice the man I used to be.

Now, don't get me wrong - there'd been a few occasions in my lifetime prior to the 'happening' when I thought I was someone else. But these times had more or less always involved the partaking of a few cheeky golden offerings to the Gods of Carlsberg. Although, there was one other time when I was on a safari in Africa and two women asked for my autograph and - while I was signing certain body parts - asked me what my inspiration was for writing the song *'500 Miles'*?

So, apart from those 1,847 occasions - not including my dishonest proclamation with a magic marker - I'd always truly believed I was just 'me'. And that there was only one of 'me'. But that was to change in a place near a coastline which remains imprinted in horror on the eyeballs of surviving members of the Luftwaffe.

Now, I've produced many short films over the past few years for a variety of clients - including NHS Mental Health Trusts - so I'm fairly familiar with the diagnosis of 'personality disorder'. It basically means a person's attitudes and behaviours are a bit different to everyone else - but not different enough to make that person eligible for a lengthy stay in Broodmoor.

So it's with certain certainty that my very own unique and extraordinary personality disorder was to come alive at the Crabble Stadium - courtesy of the Whites' late equaliser which booted our return to the Football League quest into

Wembley. And with hindsight - a great ferry town result for me and thousands of you.

But it was a scoreline which also awakened 'myself'.

Until that 88th minute Ricky Modeste header - I'm quietly confident it had always just been 'me'. But that late, late horror show was to spark the rise of 'myself' in what was the beginning of my own delicious personality disorder.

'Me' and 'myself' are the same - with one difference and one difference only. 'Me' seems to take care of all the usual and mundane aspects of everyday life. From working, finding work, paying bills and providing for my family - to making sure I'm not standing in a puddle when I'm plugging something into an electric socket. In other words - doing my best to be responsible amid the humdrum of daily life. But truly living? That's where 'myself' embraces the truly ecstatic life experience of being a Rovers supporter.

I was gutted as I slowly meandered away from the Crabble on that day in May last year, along with many others adorned in blue and white. And it was then that I realised there must have been a reason for feeling hurt? It meant I cared - cared a lot - and that meant I'd fallen in love with faithful and true. The draw had anointed me and the heartache was the ritual baptism of 'myself' as a Gashead.

'Me' and 'myself' will be forever together. One takes care of the other. 'Me' is responsible for the prosaic demands of life and ensures I keep to the speed limits on the way to the

Mem - whilst 'myself' screams at the heavens in elation and punk-pogo's with my mate Mark in the Blackthorn End when our Irish hit-man grabs a cross and smashes into the back of the net!

'Me' gets us there. 'Myself' is the explosion of emotions.

To describe it best would be to look at Leonardo da Vinci's Vitruvian Man - with 'myself' being the bloke doing the star-jump in celebration of being part of the best club in the country. I never thought I could feel this way.

I always thought it would forever just be 'me'. But now I've found 'myself' and 'myself' completes 'me' in our own twin-seat rollercoaster ride in this life.

Great times for us and we deserve it all. We deserve it because we've always given everything when we had nothing. And I know that to be true because I've been proud member of the Blue Army since that day on the 3rd of May 2014. But we followed. We defended our home. We broke away attendance records on the road. Others would have walked away. We don't and never will. We stay 'til the end - even when we have nothing. And that's what now sees us have everything.

Our potential's been seen and our potential has attracted investment by a man who sees this. Sure, it'll take time to evolve and take shape - but it's this financial acknowledgement which sees my own Vitruvian 'myself' going a bit joyously mental - whilst 'me' does his best to stop fantasising about a future BRFC captain hoisting the FA Cup aloft to the echoes of thousands-strong-songs exploding within and around Wembley.

But it's now as I write these words that I realise that 'myself' doesn't complete 'me'. There's a third. And it's her history true from which was born the traditions of then - through to the unity of now. Her name resonates in sound from whichever terrace we may stand and it was her name which called out for me to follow. Follow faithful. Follow true. And so the three of us embark on a new and incredible journey. And I know in my heart of blue that we'll be forever together...

Me, myself and Irene.

Wycombe Wanderers 1 v 0 Bristol Rovers

27th February 2016

Luke O'Nien's header for the home side in the 85th minute was the only goal of the match and the result saw Wycombe leapfrog Rovers to move into sixth in League Two - with DC's men dropping down into tenth postion.

Where's a lightning bolt when you really need one?

15 WHAT TO DO?

BRISTOL ROVERS 4 V HARTLEPOOL 1
1ST MARCH 2016

I hate January and I hate February even more than I hate January.

It's not really anything to do with the cold weather. Well, I don't think it is? I don't think it can be? I'm Scottish and I'm ginger. I'm built for the cold. Put me in snow and ice and I'm happy. Take me on holiday and I burn, blister and peel. That makes me itchy and miserable and that misery can be highly infectious to those who're on holiday with me! So I must have been a delight to be around when I was growing up in Africa. People must have seen me coming and whispered, *"Here comes that small, red, seeping, flakey, angry child again. Quick. Hide!"*

Actually, that's not strictly true. I go a lovely golden brown. But you really didn't need to know that!

I do enjoy November and December. Nice months which build up to something and then that something becomes celebrations. But January and February? No thank you. A ten month year would suit me fine thanks.

March is different. It's a move away from the grey and grim and icy skint anguish of existence. And I've just realised I may be taking this too far?

Melodrama! Quite apt, actually. The Hartlepool keeper was indulging in a wee bit of that on the first night of March at the Memorial Stadium. But how did it all happen? It happened like this...

So it was on the first day of the third month that a player who'd so far collected three yellows was to clinch another three goals for the second time since his first hat trick of the season against Wycombe in November. You might want to read that back? It's a bit late as I'm writing this and I feel as if my eyes are going to fall out. I think it makes sense. I hope it makes sense. And I really hope it does make sense because my brain at this time of night won't let me write it again. I'm either very tired or I've just become dyslexic? I hope that's the right spilleng?

So where were we? Oh yeah. Hartlepool at home and we were 3-0 up at half time. And to be honest - I really didn't know what to do with myself?

Matty Taylor opened the scoring in the 10th minute and then Gaffney decided he fancied one too. So in the 31st minute - Gaffers thought, "I think I'll have a pop at goals!" So he did. And it worked out. Then Taylor thought, "I quite fancy another one! I might use my head this time!" So he did. And it was actually good header too! And it went in. So we were 3-0 up at half time. THAT'S THREE NIL UP AT HALF TIME!

Everything seemed to be getting a bit weird. I was standing on my spot on the step in the north terrace during the interval wondering what the hell had just happened in the first half of the game?

I'd never witnessed anything like that before and so I didn't know how to feel. Sometimes it doesn't take much to leave me feeling confused.

My usual half time emotions usually involve stress, panic and terror. And I'm not talking about the chicken tikka pie! I'm talking about the feeling of dread and fear at the forthcoming prospect of grinding out a goal to clinch a late, late win and once again deny me the opportunity of having to somehow give myself mouth-to-mouth to remain in this mortal Gashead realm.

Now I mentioned this in *Faithful and True* and I remain convinced that there should be a courtesy defibrillator given to each Gashead who purchases a season ticket.

During my inaugural spell as an aspiring Gashead - I heard the same thing over and over again, *"We tend to do things the hard way!"* But because I hadn't reached maturity and was just a fledgling Blue Army foot soldier – I'd yet to feel the full impact of what that comment actually meant.

Conference. Dover. Play-offs. Wembley. Boom! It didn't take me long to experience the feelings surrounding being a proper Gashead and a massive part of that experience was watching the lads clinch late winners after ninety minutes and it was honestly the first time I could properly feel my heart doing its very best to find a way to escape from my chest as my arsehole did its best seal itself up forever.

So being 3-0 up at half time left me feeling a bit weird in as much as I didn't know what to do with myself. I did seriously think about trying one of those pastries – but a little voice within me kindly reminded me that I'd been through enough stomach churning experiences in my life and why the hell would I want to indulge in any more suffering?

So I just decided to stand and stare at our new scoreboard which was flashing with a 3-0 so bright it began to melt my eyeballs as I stuffed a Twix into my mouth to hush my gums to avoid whingeing to my friends about having nothing to whinge about - thanks to the scoreline.

Scots can be miserable. Hold on - that's not true. Let me try again. Scots are miserable and I'm no exception. But there's a reason for this and it's a simple reason…

Imagine living in a climate that's forever raining and cold? Would you be miserable? Of course you would. So there's your answer. But the climate inspires more misery than the misery which falls from the skies.

During my fourteen year stay in Scotland following my return from South Africa - it was to become part of my early morning routine to walk to the studios at Cowcaddens in the centre of Glasgow.

I'd get up. I'd have a cuppa. I'd have a shower. I'd get dressed. I'd open the front door and look out and say, "Oh for fuck's sake!"

Now I did that for years. I did that for so very long and it was always the same response from me to the bleakness which lay beyond the drawn curtains.

It never changed. It was always the same four words from that deep place within me which wanted to keep the words within as the words did their best to escape. That's how special swearing is to us. We swear because we enjoy expressing our own unique misery at having to endure that which falls from above and then freezes - an iciness which breaks bones. But fear not. We do enjoy a good sense of humour. Especially when we see someone landing on their arse. And it was the Hartlepool keeper who landed on his in the second half.

Now I have to be very careful here. I can't really mention Trevor Carson by name because he might get upset and take legal action. So I'll just refer to him as Mr Grey because that's the colour he was wearing.

Now Mr Grey did something a bit silly. His teammate Billy Paynter pulled one back for Hartlepool in the 52nd minute and this inspired Mr Grey to turn around to face us lot in the Blackthorn End to offer some kind of hand gesture to express his delight at what had just happened.

No as I mentioned earlier – this kind of behaviour is very unwise. And it's especially unwise when it's acted out only yards from where over a thousand Gasheads are standing. It's not big and it's not clever.

So Grey made his gesture and the wrath of the north terrace rained down on him with such a wrath that he must have thought he was standing in Glasgow for a few seconds.

The Blackthorn choir then delivered Newton's Third Law of Motion (for every action there is an equal but opposite reaction) to Grey and this response was bolstered by hundreds of others in song as we all sang, "It's all your fault! It's all your fault! It's all your fault, it's all your fault, it's all your fault!!"

Grey just stood with his back to us – but his right hand was slightly raised and I noticed it was shaking in some kind of weird gesture - but not as weird as the grin on his face which could be seen as he turned his head slightly towards where we were going a little bit mental.

But Grey wasn't done. It went from weird to bizarre as he slapped his own arse with his vibrating hand. And that worried me. And my concerns were courtesy of the contingent of young supporters who were bouncing up and down with middle finger digits extended towards the visiting keeper. I didn't want them to be left traumatised by a vibrating hand slapping an arse. Young minds are delicate. But then again - they seemed to be okay after witnessing Jon Parkin the previous season.

It was only a few minutes later when Matty thought, *"I fancy three. It's been a while since Morcambe last November. I fancy a tap in!"* So he did. And we all cheered and jumped up and down as Grey raced out to complain to the referee. And he stayed out there for quite a while. I don't think he could bare the thought of having to turn around because, *"It's all your fault…"* had just erupted again and it was a whole lot louder than the first time…

So it was a great night with a great result and a second great hat trick from Matty Taylor. Overall - a fantastic result and it was a result which saw us move up from 10th to 6th in the league table with 53 points.

16 NEW FACES AND ON AIR

It was to be a busy week for myself and the club.

Bristol Rovers appointed three new appointments to the
staff as the beginnings of the new infrastructure got
underway less than two weeks following the purchase of
the club by the Al-Qadi family.

New director Lee Atkins - the key figure in helping Rovers
move to the new stadium along with Michael Cunnah - the
former Chief Executive of Wembley Stadium and Finance
Director of the Football Association who would be
advising the new owners on the new stadium. And the third
new face - Will Dubey - a performance analyst from

London with expertise in football analytics who spent four years looking at games from Championship level through to Pan Asian matches.

New and highly skilled experts. Expertise which promises to deliver the best for a new future for our club - a club regarded as the best by the best supporters within the Bristol area and beyond.

And it was as one of those supporters that I was to enjoy an on-air chat with man who is nothing less than legendary in the eyes of those who follow the blue and white quarters...

Geoff Twentyman is held with high regard in these parts and it was a privilege to meet him the night following the new appointments at the Memorial Stadium.

A defender in his time - Geoff netted 6 goals during a seven year period with *'The Gas'* between 1986 and 1993 and is now a respected and prominent broadcaster with the BBC.

I was Geoff's second guest and Paul 'Punky' Randall was first in the hot seat. And when it was my turn - we talked about the book - including how the club fought back from relegation to promotion the previous season and to a new era under new ownership - a new ownership which had already begun with making new appointments to ensure a measured and careful investment of expertise and resources for the required infrastructure to guide the club towards future success.

Now I'm writing these words to explain what my experience of last season was and I really do hope you're enjoying it so far. And as I'm writing this section - right now - I'm just finding out that Geoff has once again invited me to appear on his radio show to talk about the book

'HAVING A GAS' - BBC Radio Studios 3RD March 2016

you're reading right now. And that's going to take place next week.

I'm really looking forward to seeing him again for many reasons - the first of which is to thank him in person for replying to the letter which Helen's mum wrote to him and his teammates all those years ago after the sudden death of her son, Antony.

It was only when I was doing research for this book that I found out what they'd done for Carole. So I'm truly indebted to Geoff and the other players for the support which they provided by replying to her letter.

PS: please excuse the above pic. Not sure if I look like Hannibal Lecter or Akinfenwa just before he ate his brother?

Notts County 0 v Bristol Rovers 2

5th March 2016

This is a very special day in our house. We get cake!

The reason we get cake is because it's a certain Gashead's birthday and she started going to games at Eastville - but never actually saw a match.

The never saw a game because she was the one in the van selling hotdogs and hamburgers to earn a few pennies. But she remembers hearing every single home game from her own time spent at the spiritual home of Bristol Rovers and she definitely remembers seeing the ball appear and disappear from the other side of a wall where the match was taking place...

Helen was to fall in love with the Gas during the Twerton years and as I've already mentioned - it was seeing Ollie on his knees and in tears at the end of the 1988/1989 season after reaching the third division play-off final for the first time but failing to win promotion. And she's followed ever since...

The 5th of March is her birthday and Rovers were away to Notts County with just twelve fixtures remaining in the season.

But we were a bit worried. And our concerns were justified.

As far back as Helen can remember - Rovers have never won a game on her birthday. So I'm sure you'll understand why there was genuine surprise in our house after our lads went up to Meadow Lane and returned with three points after Montano and Brown scored in the 43rd and 50th minutes respectively - a result which left the Magpies to a fifth game without victory and saw Darrell Clarke's men remain in 6th position in the league table on fifty six points.

So we lit the candles and we all sang Happy Birthday to Helen. But something didn't feel right. It didn't feel right not because it felt wrong. It didn't feel right because something felt very right.

It was around this time that I started to get the feeling that something incredible was going to happen. Now I know I'm a writer and that means I script what I see and hear. So I try and do my best to avoid clichés like 'it feels as if it's already been written'…

But that's what it felt like to me. From where I was standing - on one foot - I could feel something building and it definitely felt like 'it's already been written' and what I was feeling was also being felt by others.

It felt as if our time had arrived...

17 DON'T EAT ME

BRISTOL ROVERS 3 V WIMBLEDON 1
8TH MARCH 2016

Wombling around on a Tuesday night at the Memorial Stadium just before we played our fixture which had been postponed in February due to an Act of God - I bumped into a young man who is a proper Gashead.

I've known young Jake for a few season's now and he's a top lad with blue blood who produces his own video blogs about being a Rovers supporter. And it's not that unusual to see him pointing his mobile phone at games so that he can introduce match highlights into his blogs - blogs which are for certain ears only because if you're a bit sensitive about swearing then it's highly unlikely you'll enjoy watching his videos because when Rovers score all hell breaks loose and all you can see is the camera doing its very best to capture Venus and Jupiter and Mars as the screams of, *"Fucking get it!!!"* from Jake and his mates fills the day or night sky - depending on whether or not it's a Saturday fixture or a midweek match.

Now I've just actually spoken to him on the phone because I needed to get his permission to use his name in the book and he said no problem. So I thought - since I was chatting with him - I'd ask him if he had any funny stories from the season which I could write into this bit for him?

So I asked him and there was a long pause and after a few hums and haws he replied, *"Difficult. It tends to be a bit miserable being a Rovers supporter!"*

I almost fell off my chair laughing! But it's true!

I know we've just won back to back promotions and I'm genuinely still trying my best to take it all in - but it really does all feel like a dream and it's as if I'm just going to be floating along as the days and weeks pass until the new season begins.

I know we went up. But Jake has a valid point. I'm not saying it was easy to do. It wasn't. But in all honesty - I wasn't expecting it to happen that way. I was expecting a gruelling grind in the play-offs and to once again be truthful - I wasn't convinced we'd make it to Wembley if we were involved in the play-offs. And I say that based on what I remember I was thinking and feeling at the start of March. I genuinely had a feeling we'd go up automatically at this time.

So I bumped into Jake and we were chatting about all of this and he was convinced we'd make the play-offs. Now it's not that I didn't believe him. I believed him in as much as I had a feeling there would be success for us – but this feeling involved automatic promotion.

I remember being apprehensive about sharing what I thought and my apprehension was based on knowing we still had a fair way to go and before going into the Wombles match - we remained nine points adrift of the top three.

But I said it anyway. It felt right and it felt strong. So I said, *"I reckon we'll go up automatically. We'll finish third!"*

The words just came out and I'm glad they did. Not because of any reason to do with what actually happened. It's just what I believed at the time. I can also be a bit superstitious too. I didn't want to ruin everything by stating what I thought. It's as if there's a wee part of me which says, *"Say it and you'll fuck it all up!"*

And fuck it up was the last thing I wanted. More than anything else in the world - I wanted to see us go up. And I genuinely felt it was our time. It's the only way I can describe it. And I know there were many others who felt the same - but just didn't want to utter the words for fear of being denied what had already been decided by the Gods of Football.

So we were at home to Wimbledon with twelve games to go and it was Jermaine Easter who nodded Rovers ahead from Lee Brown's cross before Ollie Clarke doubled the lead with a low right-footed shot which saw us 2-0 up at the interval.

Jon Meades scored with a header in the 52nd minute for the Wombles - but our hitman Taylor put the game well beyond them after he scored his 19th goal of the season to clinch the three points.

Wimbledon decided to throw everything they had at the game in an attempt to try and save face. They introduced Ade Akinfenwa in the 80th minute but he was red-carded ten minutes later for dissent.

And it was this point that I saw something take place in the Blackthorn End which I'd never witnessed before. The young'uns who stand at the front and who usually take great pleasure in barracking dismissed visiting players - hid behind the boarding.

Not surprising really. They knew they were within easy reach of Akinfenwa as he bounced off the pitch and so they must have known that meant they were within an arm's reach of becoming a starter. Albeit it tends to be an arm which he generally enjoys before his main course.

So it finished 3-1 to Rovers and the result saw us move up into 5th position on fifty nine points and the gap between ourselves and the top three was reduced to six.

Northampton were sitting in poll position on seventy eight points with second placed Oxford and third placed Plymouth both on sixty fives. It looked highly unlikely that anyone was going to topple the Cobblers but the vying for the remaining two automatics looked destined to be a dogfight and it was already being discussed amongst supporters that the final day of the season could very well be one to remember.

And it was at this very time that a reminder of what happened last season was to appear on Twitter. Lee Mansell had tweeted something similar in our run-in to Wembley with eleven games still to play. The same was happening twelve months later and as soon as the tweet hit the ether - it was shared far and wide by Bristol Rovers supporters.

Lee Mansell @manse7   08/03/2016
11 to go you never know ⚽⚽⚽
          ↻ 148   ♥ 312   ✉

This wasn't just a tweet. This was a rally call for all to get behind the lads by remembering what had happened the season before. Sent down in May in 2014 - the almost impossible was to be achieved twelve months later.

Now, was it possible to achieve the unimaginable? Back to back promotions?

'11 to go you never know' could be seen and heard everywhere. Mansell's words announced the run in. He believed it. I'm sure his teammates and gaffer believed it. Now Gasheads were beginning to believe it too. And why the hell not!!

18 LIVING THE DREAM

It was around this time that panic stations were sounded in my own personal life following my work coming to a standstill.

I'd received no commissions for almost seven months and it was at this point that I had to try and get work doing anything I could to bring some money into our home.

I had responsibilities to look after and the collapse of public funding had had a direct effect on the budgets of the organisations which had been hiring me to make them promotional films for several years.

I'd been waiting and waiting for work to make itself known. It had always happened this way because I'd always been commissioned through word of mouth – thanks to my rates. And I'd like to think because of the quality of my work too. But it didn't happen despite my best efforts to promote what I can do and how my work can help to market companies to attract funding for them.

No one was spending. Budgets were closed and so I went into the centre of Bristol and spent a few days handing my CV into every job agency in the city. And it didn't take long to realise that my CV was actually working against me. No demand for a forty eight year old former television producer/director/journalist/author/documentary filmmaker/promo maker. And it didn't really surprise me to be honest. But I did need to find work and I needed to find it quickly. But it was proving very difficult…

Now there's a very good reason as to why I'm sharing this with you. I suppose part of the reason is as I've mentioned before - being a Gashead isn't just about the football for me. It's a huge part of my life and if there are other parts of my life which aren't going very well - then it can have an effect on me going to games.

My first and foremost responsibility is to provide for my family and that will always be paramount. But it was a brand new experience to have to think that I wouldn't be able to go to matches anymore because of my financial situation. And that scared the shit into me!

Knowing a game was going on at the Mem and not being able to be there would hurt. So I just buckled down and got prepared to do anything at all to earn a bit of money.

I'm not a proud man. I'll do anything to provide for those I love. But not Morris dancing. Fuck that. There are limits!

I've been through enough over the years and it's helped me to see things in another way. Sure, I may have to clean toilets or any other kind of job that no one else wants to do. But when you've had to suffer losing absolutely everything and everyone in your life and you've almost lost your life - that experience gives you a unique perspective on life itself. And that perspective is this - things can never be that bad. But you have to experience 'that bad' first before you realise just how good cleaning toilets can be...

I didn't end up cleaning toilets in the end. Oh no. It was much worse than that. Cleaning toilets would have been a luxury!

I joined a job agency which put people into work in the industrial sector. Factory work and warehouse work and driver's mate work was what was available. And my first job was working twelve hour shifts in a medical waste incineration facility in Avonmouth. Lush.

The shift involved me and another poor bastard having to empty hospital waste from a container the size of a small African nation and empty the delights into huge yellow bins and wheel them up to another level where they were all lined up to be destroyed by fire. At one point I did actually think I was working in Hell. Then again - pushing squidgy body parts around at 4am is Hell! Unless you're a serial killer!

The container was massive and it was rammed with goodies and a lot of the goodies were seeping and bubbling and not really pleasant on the nose.

I was given armoured clothing and gloves. I was also given a mask. Some may say that's a good thing.

This left me a bit fearful. But I was informed that I had no need to worry. They'd done their best - when packing the container - to make sure all syringes and needles were removed. But if I did feel a prick - then I should let them know straight away and they'd rush me to hospital and I'd be well looked after. Although they did say that if this did happen - then I'd be unable to have any kind of human contact for six months until I got the all clear of being clear of every known life-threatening infection known to man.

But I did feel a prick and when I asked if I could get armoured trousers which fitted properly - instead of the ones which were too big and made me complete the image of looking like a killer clown - they told me I looked fine. But I knew they were lying!

The night was slow and long and exhausting. It was also putrid and foul and wet. But I did it and I lasted through the night. And what drove me to get to the end of the shift was thinking about my family and thinking about how one hour of working in the shithole would almost earn me a match ticket. I could live with that...

I only did one shift and packed it in at 6am. But I did stay 'til the end. I found out afterwards that not many stay until the shift is over. Most walk away after a few hours. But I started it and I finished it and I was always going to stay 'til the end.

The following day I was offered some shifts at a panel cutting warehouse in Fishponds. I took it and I'm still getting a fair amount of work there to this day.

The job I'm doing is mind-numbingly boring. But it's money and the guys who work there are fantastic. One is a City fan and one is a Swindon supporter. The other guy is just crazy. And that's why we call him 'Crazy John'! But he wasn't always crazy. He used to be a semi-pro darts player who once played against Barneveld. He lost. Maybe that's what tipped him over the edge?

Phil the Shithead (that's how he's listed in my phone) said to me once, *"You Gasheads know how to enjoy yourselves - don't you? We just fight each other. But you lot seem to have a lot of fun when you're at home or away!"*

Phil's way too switched-on and cool to be one of them. He even knows how to use a spoon and we do have a great laugh together chatting about football and other things - including whether or not Crazy John is actually crazy?

I think he might be up for turning? We'll see…

But Phil's bang-on! We do have a lot of fun. And there was a whole lot more fun to be had following our 3-1 win over Wimbledon.

19 WELCOME BACK

BRISTOL ROVERS 1 V MANSFIELD 0
12TH MARCH 2016

Mansfield was a big one for me...

I knew it wasn't their fault. They just did what they did.
The damage had been done earlier in the 2013/2014
season. But this game was a big one for me.

As you now know - it was witnessing the events of that day
at our ground twenty four months ago which was to see the
beginning of my own calling to follow the Gas. And so I
wrote something before the match kicked-off:

'From hurt to absolution - that will be my thought as we wander up Strathmore Road and pass the Victorian rows as we head towards the Memorial Stadium to face Mansfield.

Mansfield. Home town of our gaffer and the side which hand delivered the final nail in our 2013/2014 coffin. But so much has happened since that day and now we face them for the first time at our ground since that awful May afternoon almost two years ago. Mansfield...

They weren't to blame. They did their job. And with hindsight - it seems as if they did us a favour? But don't get me wrong - I'd never wish for that kind of favour again. Ever. But what was to follow was incredible.

From the Blue Army siege at the gates of Woking to the Dover draw to the Taylor 'Worm' amid the undulating scenery in Nailsworth to Mansell at Wembley to the return to where we belong. And now look at us - just six points off second spot with a manager and squad to be proud of at the start of a new era in our history following the arrival of Wael Al-Qadi and Steve Hamer and a growing entourage which promises to lay the foundation of successes to come.

From hurt to absolution - that's what I'll be thinking of and that's what I'll be proud of as we turn right off Strathmore and onto Filton Avenue to make our way into the place where we watch the team that means the world to us. Bristol Rovers FC.

Many never return from where we've been. But none are like us. Events of the past twenty two months prove that - events which have witnessed a unity reborn and stoked with fight and heart and tradition and history.

Memorial Stadium 3 May 2014

Mansfield - we're ready for you now...

That day in that May is no more. We're here now and we mean business. We're not the same as the last time you faced us in our place. And we're looking forward to welcoming you to our new time.

I'll have no resentments or grudges as I stand on my spot in the North Terrace at 3pm this Saturday. Instead - I'll be a Gashead proud. And my pride will fill when I hear fellow supporters cry out in song as our gaffer's men escort the visitors out of our tunnel and into the roar of Irene as she welcomes them in song - an anthem old but new in fight and heart and passion.

I made a decision yesterday. The sequel to *Faithful and True, A Gashead's Story* will feature these words. It just feels right to me.

It feels right because it was while watching Gasheads holding tightly onto the steel gates on that day that I began to feel something for the club. Something deep. Something very real. And that 'something' grew into love during the following season's Conference campaign and that will never leave me.

From hurt to absolution. Darrell Clarke and his squad have given us that. And I don't mid saying I think I'll have a few tears of pride in the Blackthorn End just before three o'clock this Saturday. UTG!'

There was just something about this game which – for me – was signaling something was going on and that something was sending us signs that this was indeed our time.

It was Darrell Clarke's 100th match in charge of Rovers and it was against the side from his home town.

Matty Taylor's 60th minute strike saw him reach his twenty goal tally and the win made it four successive victories for the Gas.

It was by no means a great game and if it wasn't for Steve Mildenhall - a Lee Collins late effort could have seen a very different result. But once again the Rovers keeper was proving his worth and it was a worth worth seeing as game after game passed with our keeper proving he may not be one of our own - but he certainly is one of our own.

The result saw DC's men sitting fourth in League Two on sixty two points and just three points below joint second and third - Oxford and Plymouth.

Everything seemed to be moving up a gear now. We were just not getting into the automatic spots below Northampton - but many believed that was okay. There was still plenty of time to move up. Better to snap at the heels than have your heels snapped. Just sit beneath them and wait for one of them to slip up.

Four in a row with ten to go. You just never know.

20 FATTY DISGUISE

NEWPORT 1 V BRISTOL ROVERS 4
19TH MARCH 2016

It was just one of those times when you see a player pick up the ball and run like hell with it and you know he has the full intention of burying it past the keeper and into the net!

And that's what Ollie Clarke did in the 15th minute against Warren Feeney's side at Rodney Parade.

We were all standing in an away end which was doing its best to impersonate scaffolding on a building site when we all saw Ollie and it was very clear what his intention was thirteen minutes after Newport's Alex Rodman opened the scoring.

It may have been the first goal but it wasn't the last of the match - although all the rest came from Darrel Clarke's side.

Our visit to the land of song and dragon came just two days after Bristol Rovers' appeal in the legal battle against Sainsbury's was quashed by three Appeal Court judges. But to be honest - the once hot topic for desperate conversation had died a quick and sudden death following the arrival of Wael Al Qadi and new chairman Steve Hamer.

Both men assured supporters that they would indeed enjoy a new stadium in the near future and that a new ground was paramount in the implementation of the new club infrastructure within the new vision of 'evolution not revolution'.

So we simply trusted them and we still do. And with that in mind it wasn't really on our minds as we paid our toll at the Severn Bridge and prepared for a day of fun with the choral locals.

The highlight of the whole day has completely nothing to do with the game. Don't get me wrong - the match was incredible - but hearing Helen shout out loud, *"Tideeee!"* when I stopped the car at a Welsh Harvesters for breakfast just cracked me up! Helen loves sausage.

So there were a few of us, including our mates Claire and Simon and their lad - Dan.

Now Dan is a bit of a football nut and he's a top bloke. He's also a very good young and aspiring football writer and he used to write material for Gascast. And I'd say he's probably the best young writer I've seen around for a long time.

He writes from his head and his heart. So many just copy styles which they've read for years. It's so cliched. But Dan puts a lot of himself into what he writes about the game.

He takes a risk. He puts himself 'out there'. I respect that and for me - that's what makes him stand out. He's got his own blog on the go at the moment. He's worth a look. Dan Ball. Apart from that - he's a bit of an exhibitionist.

We arrived outside his house one day to pick him up for a game at the Mem. He wasn't ready. He was still wandering around the house - naked!

Now it's at this point that I need to point out that he told us he was starkers. I didn't peek through his window. He told us and that means he put it in the public domain and that means I can write about it without any legal action being taken. I didn't peer through any windows. I haven't done that for months now...

So we gorged ourselves on a Welsh English breakfast and then rolled along towards Rodney Parade. And there was no problem walking to the ground after we parked the car. The Newport casuals just let us wobble past. No trouble at all. But my confusion abated once I realised they probably thought we were locals. And that was courtesy of our size - after eating the Welsh English breakfast.

Gasheads celebrate Matty Taylor's goal at Rodney Parade

So Ollie netted a tidy strike in the first half which saw mayhem erupt in our away end with over one thousand members of the Blue Army going mental. And we were to enjoy the same experience over and over and over again as Montano and Taylor and Harrison hit true to see the final score finish 4-1 to us lot and the sight of Darrell coming over to us at the end and fists clenched in a gesticulation of *"Come on!"* is an image I'll be proud to remember for a long time!

Five wins out of five in March and Bristol Rovers move into the automatic promotion spots - sitting third on sixty five points behind Oxford who are on seventy one.

Jordan flag at Rodney Parade - 19th March 2016

21 CLOSENESS

It was following the win at Newport that Darrell Clarke talked about the togetherness within his squad. And that night I wrote this:

'They sense it and they see it. I saw it at Rodney Parade and I'm convinced I saw it when we were at home to Wimbledon two weeks ago. The opposition senses it too as they see it and it's as if there's nothing they can do about it.

I mean no disrespect to other teams. That's never my intention because I know that the next nine games will be more like cup ties and each and every encounter will be a hard fight. But I truly believe our team has found a newer and inspired resolve which eludes many others in this league - a depth of will and determination which broadens shoulders to carry the burden of purpose, even when they're a goal down.

Belief. More than just the desire to win. More like players finding something deep within themselves which tells them they WILL win and so they DO win.

That belief doesn't come easy. That belief is nurtured and grown over time by a management team which truly believes in the individual purpose of each and every player. They see it. They guide it. They inspire it to grow.

Darrell Clarke talks about a 'togetherness' in his squad and this bond is now clearly evident. Five consecutive wins is testament to his words as his team's 'closeness' cements every player together in one single purpose. Win.

Togetherness delivers strength in coming together to get the job done and once this closeness is tempered by belief in self and belief in the team - then something very special can happen.

The opposition senses it. The opposition sees it. It's not as if they lie down. They wouldn't. This is a highly competitive league and no team gives up. But once a togetherness in purpose catches alight on the pitch - you can see the opposition flounder slightly as they become aware that they're up against a unity of depth in belief. And that's difficult to play against if you haven't got it.

Clarke's squad has it. They went to Rodney Parade - unbeaten in four - and took on a side which had recently travelled to Portsmouth and gave them a hiding. But the pounders of Pompey were up against a side which fields a team bound by togetherness. And the result was a 4-1 away win for the blue and white quarters.

They sense it and they see it. And now they know it. They know it because Clarke has mustered a selection of players who, in his own words, *'stick together as a group'* and it's clear they now have the mentality and the closeness to face the nine game siege which begins on Good Friday. Time to batten down the hatches because this is going to be one helluva ride!

Cambridge are next and the holiday clash at the Memorial Stadium is likely to attract a huge crowd - because there are others who see it and sense it too. Gasheads. One thousand travelled to Newport. We stood together and our sound silenced the choir of Exiles. Banished are the days of uncertainty following win after win and events off the pitch are playing a part too. New owner. New chairman. New infrastructure. New future. Rovers supporters are seeing it all and sensing it too. Happy Days indeed.

'Nine to go you never know!' Lee Mansell speaks the truth. We don't know for sure because the run-in will be tough. But what we do know is there's a togetherness within the squad and there's a closeness amid the supporters too. The opposition sees it. We see it. The gaffer knows it and the players believe in it. Cambridge – we look forward to you seeing it too! And Gaffney says hello!'

'And the light of sun fell down on the Blackthorn End as hands reached for the sky amid the echoes of Irene'

22 HE'S OURS NOW

He was substituted after seventy nine minutes and as he made his way off the pitch - over ten thousand Bristol Rovers supporters erupted into song, *"Oh Rory Gaffney you are the love of my life. Oh Rory Gaffney I'd let you shag my wife. Oh Rory Gaffney I want ginger hair too!"*

It was an affirmation in sound to the man who'd played an important part in denying his former club any chance of getting a foothold in a game which saw Rovers 2-0 up after eighteen minutes - courtesy of two Billy Bodin strikes.

Bodin's first came after nine minutes with a low drive from twenty five yards. His second - a header from a Danny

Leadbitter near-post cross and the goal was to see the midfielder take his tally to eight for the season.

Matty Taylor decided he wanted in on the action too and after the interval he slotted one past U's keeper Will Norris in the 73rd minute to keep Rovers third in League Two on sixty eight points. But only on goal difference above fourth placed Plymouth.

The dogfight was well underway. Only Northampton looked safe regarding realising aspirations for League One football during the 2016/2017 campaign.

The rest was pretty much still up for grabs with only twelve points separating seventh from second with eight to go. Who wanted it most?

By the time the Irish striker had left the pitch - the song from the ten thousand confirmed the inevitability of the result as the sound of *"He left coz you're shit. He left coz you're shit! Rory Gaffney he left coz you're shit!"* echoed around the Memorial Stadium.

Rovers were flying high and it was a good Friday for Gasheads in a week which also saw the appointment of two new Honorary Vice Presidents in former Chairman Geoff Dunford and ex-Director Rod King.

Carlisle 3 v Bristol Rovers 2

28th March 2016

It was an uprising in the 85th minute in Cumbria which put a stop to Rovers' winning run to deny Darrell Clarke's side a sixth successive win.

The Gas came from behind twice in the game through Bodin and Taylor - but Kennedy ran onto a through ball and calmly lifted it over the head of Mildenhall with only five minutes remaining.

A long way to go and a longer drive back for those who travelled. Applause for those who did. And the result saw Rovers drop out of the automatic spots and into fifth position - still on sixty eight points.

23 BIRTHDAY BOOM!

BRISTOL ROVERS 3 V CRAWLEY TOWN 0
2ND APRIL 2016

The 2nd of April was to be a day of surprises for someone who I regard as a true friend.

He had no idea of what awaited him at the Memorial Stadium just five days before his 50th birthday and that's because he wasn't going to be watching from his usual spot from the Blackthorn End. Oh no!

As a special birthday surprise - his wife had arranged with the club that he could in fact.......wait for it........be Captain Gas for the day!!!

Okay, okay - I'm kidding. But there was a surprise for
Simon and he was going to be watching the match from
one of the VIP hospitality suites in the main stand - just
along the corridor from where Wael watches the game.

He had no idea. I had my main work camera with me and I
told him the club had allowed me to use it to get some
decent fans shots. But it was actually to film the birthday
celebrations in his honour.

I remember offering him another pint just before the
match behind the Blackthorn End. It was a beautiful sunny
spring day and a pint was definitely a must. Although I
decided to stick with a couple of J2Os. It's much better that
way as you now know.

These days I just say I'm allergic to alcohol if someone I
don't know offers me a pint. The reaction tends to be
something like, *"Really? Never heard of that before?"* To which
I usually reply, *"Yeah. If I drink I break out in handcuffs!"*

So I asked Simon if he fancied another Golden Offering to
the Gods? He said no thanks. He just fancied only one
because him and Claire were going to New York for a few
days to celebrate his birthday. And it would likely involve
lots of eating and drinking - so he thought he'd take it easy
on his body for two days before indulging in a food and
alcohol orgy in the Big Apple for six days.

Four hours later - he pretty much crawled out of the Mem!
But we'll get to that in a bit...

Time passed and more and more of Simon's close friends
arrived and joined us behind the north terrace. Nothing

unusual in that you might think? Well, most of the people who were arriving never usually came to the games and they were just turning up - giving Simon a big hug - and then behaving as if they'd been Gasheads for years.

But Simon didn't seem to think anything was unusual and he just carried on chatting and sipping his pint. And I suppose with everything that was fm going on - on and off the pitch - it's fair to say that crowds were on the up with more and more people wanting to be part of all the excitement surrounding the run in to the end of the season.

And it was exciting. It was very exciting and yet there was also a sense of apprehension. Everything just seemed a bit too good to be true? We couldn't really believe it was all happening. It really wasn't that long ago since we were standing on the steps of the north terrace - many in tears following the sending down. And now all of this? A side challenging in the play-off spots challenging for automatic promotion. New owner. New chairman. New future. It just seemed too good to be true? And as we stood in the sun - Simon still oblivious to what was going on - we had absolutely no idea that it wasn't just going to be an exciting end to our season. It was going to be an end of season like no other!

So the man who misses nothing was informed about his VIP birthday gift and he was delighted! And we all headed towards the main stand to enjoy some food and cake and drinks while watching the match against Crawley and it was a game which was to deliver a second half which will be difficult to forget - thanks to one stunning free kick and three eruptions of elation as Rovers clinched yet another win at home.

Wael, Lee, Simon and Stu

Goalless at the interval - our birthday bash was to receive a welcome gate-crash by Wael, Lee Mansell and Stu Sinclair.

The three presented Simon with a shirt and a ball. They asked him to hurry up and change into the shirt because Darrell wanted to present him with boots and the rest of his kit in the dressing room.

Mansell asked Simon if he'd be up for twenty minutes - to which the birthday boy replied, *"I'm usually only up for five!"*

So with that - word was relayed down to the gaffer and Clarke had to make do with the lads he already had on the bench. Pity. I reckon five minutes of a six-pint-Simon playing up front with Taylor would be a football highlight the world would enjoy watching over and over again.

So the second half kicked off and it was Taylor who opened the scoring in the 53rd minute from a Liam Lawrence corner - and it was the former Shrewsbury Town player who delivered the free kick of the season eighteen minutes later.

His strike from twenty five yards was simply exquisite! Crawley keeper Callum Preston didn't stand a chance as Lawrence's peach hit the top left hand corner of the net. It was an absolute stormer and the Memorial Stadium just exploded in sound as over ten thousand Gasheads revelled in what they'd just witnessed - one of those goals which is possible from set play but you're not sure if it'll find its target. And when it does - it's a beauty!

Taylor wasn't done and he thought, *"I fancy a second today!"* So he then headed a second header - this time from a Chris Lines corner and that was that! Job done and there was no comeback for Mark Yates' side.

The result was to see Rovers return to the automatics in the league table with seventy one points - but only on goal difference. Two other teams were also on the same number of points. Plymouth were sitting fourth and Accrington were fifth as they began announcing their own intentions for a top three ending to the season.

As for endings - Simon's best mate Ian collected the now 'wobbling' half-centurion from the hospitality box and marched him up towards Gloucester Road to indulge in a 'proper' birthday celebration as recent memories of Goodnight Irene still echoed as Goodnight Simon began...

24 MEM EXPLOSION

NORTHAMPTON 2 V BRISTOL ROVERS 2
9TH APRIL 2016

'How does it come to this? It's as if the Gods of the
Beautiful Game have already written the script as you
scream and dance in joy - when only a few moments ago
you were in such an awful place within yourself and
surrounded by eleven hundred other supporters who were
probably feeling the same. Highs and lows.

From that uncomfortable churning inside you - to the
elation and relief in believing it's still on following an 88th
minute equaliser which wrenched a point from a side who
are now guaranteed promotion. And it's not just a point.
That one point could become priceless in the weeks to
come...

How does it come to this - when all different kinds of people from all different walks of life, come together to share in the highs and lows of a passion which is shared amid the countless differences? Togetherness in the hurt. Togetherness in the elation. Togetherness in the following. Togetherness in the love of Bristol Rovers.

How does it come to this - when we barely know one another and yet we follow and we follow without question? Hearts filled with the desire to follow 'til the end...

So how does it come to this?

This is history. This is tradition. This is generations of fight and heart embracing a unity in faithful and true. This is Bristol Rovers FC. This is Gashead!'

I wrote those words just hours after watching our away match against Northampton and it was the day which saw the Cobblers clinch promotion to League One.

The game was one of the most stressful matches I've ever had the pleasure of watching and we were with over a thousand other supporters at the Memorial Stadium as the Sixfields clash was beamed back live to our ground.

It was Nicky Adams who put the home side into an early lead before teammate Sam Hoskins side-footed a second just four minutes into the second half. And at this point - the atmosphere in the supporters' bar at the Mem was nothing less than awful.

It was one of those moments in time when you can't bare to look at the screen and so you find yourself gazing down at the carpet - not daring to look up but knowing full well that you will look up - and you do!

So I peeked upwards and once again it was Matty Taylor with a cheeky back heel which put us back in the game in the 76th minute from a Danny Leadbitter pass, And I'm still convinced our striker could hear the noise which erupted from Filton Avenue when he found the back of the net.

So it was 2-1 with two minutes to go when up popped Ellis to receive a Lee Brown pass and he tapped it in at the far corner. BOOM!

It's a bit difficult to actually explain what it felt like when the Mem exploded. So the best I can do is this - just imagine the loudest noise possible and you're hearing it as you're jumping around in nothing less than sheer ecstasy. That should pretty much cover it!

It was an incredible result to walk away from and as we departed the ground - it felt like we were walking away from a stunning victory. And in many ways - we probably were walking away from a stunning victory because every single point was priceless as the run-in approached its final straight and that value was felt and heard by Gasheads at home and those who'd travelled to Sixfields.

The draw saw us dropping down into fourth on seventy two points - just two points below Accrington who were in third.

Five to go you never know...

Bristol Rovers supporters just one second before the Harrison equaliser

Bristol Rovers supporters one second after the Harrison equaliser

25 LOST TRIBE

BRISTOL ROVERS 2 V YEOVIL 1
16 TH APRIL 2016

We were on holiday in Cyprus last August when Ellis Harrison netted the 88th minute winner against one hundred and thirty two fingers at Huish - so I was really looking forward to watching this one at our ground.

Once again I was doing my very best to get the attention of local media in the hope someone might consider offering me some freelance work - since I did have a lot of broadcasting experience following my many years with Scottish Television in Glasgow.

So I wrote a match preview in an attempt to show I still hadn't lost it and I still maintained the magic:

'It's location can only be described as somewhere near the arse end of nowhere!

It's a place which was once ravaged by plague and fire and it's a place where inhabitants once threw their morning ablutions out of their windows before heading to the town square to indulge in the daily entertainment of witch trials and shaving monkeys.

But all of that was to change at the start of 2016 when undercover animal rights activists exposed the outrage being committed against our simian chums and the outcome was to see an array of public health authorities enter the 'arse end of nowhere' and stamp out the abominations which were taking place in the middle of 'somewhere'. But it seems the damage has been done and may never be undone!

World renowned anthropologists have been trying to figure out how something like this could go unnoticed for hundreds of years - trying to get to the bottom of how the 'arse end of nowhere' managed to fall off the evolutionary wagon.

But it seems finding a hairy chimp's bottom will be a lot easier than finding the bottom of the beginning of the 'arse end of nowhere'!

But some clues to the origins of Yeovil have been uncovered. It seems the marshy surroundings played a significant part the its isolation from moving forward. Backwards was thus inevitable and the consequences ravaged everyday life - including family affairs - which became the norm.

Experts in the marshy fields believe consequences of this particular horror may take generations to disappear - but the mental torment of the inhabitants may take longer in being remedied.

This became clear on the first-ever school day when volunteers tried to teach local youngsters the song, *'One finger one thumb'!*

The outcome was carnage. But the experts believe that if they keep moving - progress might me made in 'somewhere'. And this could be true. It does seem that there is one dim light which shines from this particular dark hole at the arse end of nowhere.

It seems that deliverance has arrived in the shape of music. The natives seem to have a natural ability with string instruments and a eureka moment ensued.

An overseas medical student from Alabama had her banjo stolen and the theft has been hailed as a success! The harmonic plucking of gut (not human entrails as was the first thought) was to arise from a nearby swamp and so the thief with the stolen banjo was found. And hell - could that boy play a tune! And soon all the locals were playing. Not just playing - but playing well!

It was the breakthrough that was needed! A form of communication between civilization and the forgotten inhabitants of the arse end of nowhere! And it's now hoped that a choir may soon be added to the banjo orchestra. But only once foreign aid signs off the budget for 45,000 sets of dentures. The miracle of being discovered still doesn't guarantee the miracle of being able to sing without teeth!

It's going to take time. Lots of time. Taking it slow with the slow is a slow process. But stranger things have happened. Okay - maybe not this strange. But in time they may catch up. They may see the very tail end of civilisation and reach out. But whether they can grasp hold of it is another question.

If they do manage to hold on - then the enormity of the void may just be too much. They've been absent for so long and yet certain aspects of life and living have always been with them during their 'period of lost'.

Time. Birth. Death. Truth. Consequences. Karma. And it's the latter which may see them awaken to the truth that it might have been better if they'd never been found.

Let's hope they find that out today. UTG RTID'

My match preview - sent to many different media outlets - didn't go down very well. But what was well received was the opportunity for a packed Memorial Stadium to say hello to a certain Yeovil supporter who'd held up a certain home-made sign a few seasons ago.

But he was nowhere to be found anywhere near or around Filton Avenue. Funny that…

So the cries of, *"Where's the wanker with the sign?"* from thousands and thousands of blue and white faithful during our game against Yeovil went unanswered and all that could be heard from the attending mass from Huish was the occasional sound of gut being plucked. And we're still not sure how they managed to get their intended sacrifice victim past our security at the turnstiles.

Gaffney was outstanding in this game and he opened the scoring with a close range header from a Bodin free kick.

Yeovil equalised in the 73rd minute courtesy of Leroy Lita - but Bristol Rovers' top scorer decided he'd like his goal tally for the season to be at least twenty seven and it was in the 77th minute that he acquired his new desire.

Overall a convincing win for Darrell Clarke's men and the result saw Rovers return to an automatic spot in third place on seventy five points – ahead of Accrington on goal difference.

So we were back in the top three of League Two following a game which saw Matty Taylor score in his eighth consecutive game. And it was the match weekend which saw Northampton Town crowned as League Two Champions following a goalless draw away to Exeter.

Four to go you never know…

Stevenage 0 v Bristol Rovers 0

19th April 2016

It was a Tuesday night and Helen and I were both sitting in Southmead A&E after Beth spilled a kettle filled with boiling water all over her thigh.

So while she was being treated with potions and probed with fingers in latex gloves - we both sat in the waiting room and watched our away match against Stevenage live on Facebook.

Yes. Live on Facebook!

Hats off to the Gashead who managed to hold his phone

up for ninety minutes. There's an advantage to having a numb hand and arm - but I couldn't possibly reveal that within these pages because this is a family publication. So you'll have to use your own imagination.

And I'm afraid that's about as exciting as this report gets. A goalless draw. Accident and Emergency. Masturbation. I've had worse nights to be honest.

But it was a point. And it was to turn out to be a very, very important point even though we dropped out of the automatic spot and into fifth on seventy six points.

Three to go…

26 SING LOUD

BRISTOL ROVERS 3 V EXETER 1
23 RD APRIL 2016

For love nor money - you couldn't get a ticket for this match!

It was on and everyone knew it was on. Sure - it was still arithmetically possible for it not to be on. But that feeling still remained and that feeling for me was that it was indeed on and this was going to be one helluva end to the season.

A play-off place was now in the bag but manager Darrell Clarke made the call to supporters to get right behind the team in a rally cry which was clear to all that he believed his side had what it took to go up automatically:

"It is certainly our biggest game since the play-off final last year and we need everybody right behind us. If you're not usually a singer get singing and if you're a quiet fan - get loud!"

Rovers - just one point behind Oxford United and Plymouth Argyle who occupied third and fourth respectively - were just two points behind second-placed Accrington Stanley with three games of the season remaining.

It was definitely on. The gaffer new it and believed it. He wanted us to know it and believe it too and his belief had become infectious.

The apprehensions - based on whatever happened or didn't happen in the past - were beginning to abate. It was on if we wanted it badly enough and we so badly wanted it. And it was starting to sink in that this was indeed our time!

Bodin opened the scoring in the thirteenth minute with a strike just inside the eighteen yard box. And it was to be 2-0 at the interval following a stunning Lee Brown free kick from twenty yards in the fourth added minute of injury time.

Everyone was going mental! It just seemed to be getting better and better and Claire was so happy she actually took a photograph of the new women's toilets which had recently arrived courtesy of our new owners. I know it's a bit random. But we all express our joy in many different ways. And my delight was to actually see the inside of a ladies toilet. I know you'll not believe me - but I've never ever seen the inside of a ladies toilet. Promise!

Claire gave me a photo of the inside of the new loo. I asked her for it to use in this book. But I just can't bring myself to put it in? I must have some kind of 'decency compass'? And that's quite surprising for me!

Jake Taylor pulled one back for the visitors just after the break - but it was at that point that our very own Taylor thought, *"No way I can let that Taylor be the only Taylor on the scoreboard this afternoon!"*

So Matty banged in his 28th goal of the season and that was that! Signed. Sealed. Delivered. Three points thank you very much and it was a result which saw us move up to fourth on seventy nine points – with just two points between us and second placed Accrington! And Oxford were sitting second on eighty!

Two to go you never know…

York 1 v Bristol Rovers 4

30th April 2016

We needed someone to do us a favour...

With just two match weekends remaining in League Two - the dogfight was well and truly on for the two remaining automatic spots.

Accrington and Oxford were both getting in our way - sitting second and third respectively in the league table. So we needed one of them to slip up!

The Lancashire side were on eighty one points. The men from Kassam on eighty points. Rovers in fourth on seventy nine. It was time for someone to do us a favour!

Oxford were away to Carlisle and with the Cumbrian side having lost their previous two encounters at home - it looked more likely that the visitors could clinch points at

Brunton Park.

Accrington were away to Wycombe Wanderers - a side unbeaten at home in their previous two fixtures - so all Gashead eyes were gazing on Adams Park in the hope that the home side could deliver a result which would deny Stanley points.

We were away to York and once again we watched the game at the Memorial Stadium courtesy of another beam back and to be honest - I think most of the supporters in the club's bars were watching their mobile phones as opposed to watching our own match on the big screens. And we didn't have to wait long for the first result to alert devices all around our ground.

Oxford were awarded a penalty in the fourth minute of their game at Brunton Park. And that pretty much confirmed our pre-match speculation of what may or may not take place elsewhere. So even though we continued to monitor what was happening in Cumbria — it was generally all eyes on Adams Park. And all eyes remained on that match because it remained 0-0 for a long time.

Meanwhile in York - our lads had taken the lead in the 19th minute courtesy of Billy Bodin. And to be honest - once he hit the back of the net we were quietly confident that three points were ours for the taking. And we weren't wrong - because Bodin struck again in the 71st minute and at that point the scores were York 0-2 Bristol Rovers; Wycombe 0-0 Accrington; Carlisle 0-Oxford 1.

Three minutes after Billy's second goal - Oxford scored again at Brunton and that ruled out any slip-up there. So we continued to monitor the match being played at Adams Park and it was in the 78th minute that Stanley scored. So nothing changed. The three sides occupying second, third and fourth remained in second, third and fourth in the league table – so we were praying for an equalizer.

Easter and Mansell both scored towards the end of our own game and it was at this time when something really bizarre happened.

We were obviously watching our game on the big screen as well as keeping a check on the Adams Park match - when we heard a loud cheer come from the Gasheads who were at the ground in York. It was clear and it was very loud - so everyone in the Mem bars started tapping apps in their own mobile phones and there was even a loud cheer in the area where we were sitting. But then it all went very quiet.

I was furious. I couldn't find any result anywhere which indicated that Wycombe had scored. No one else could verify it either. And the confusion reigned for quite some time - even after the games came to an end. Some said a goal had been scored by Wycombe - but that it had been disallowed. But there was no mention of anything on results sites.

So that's how it all ended and it was now down to the final fixture list of the season to see who would clinch an automatic play-off spot and join Northampton in League One for the 2016/2017 season.

One to go you never know…

27 ROAR OF THE ROVERS

BRISTOL ROVERS 2 V DAGENHAM 1
7TH MAY 2016

I remember and I will always remember…

The memories of that day remain all mixed up in my mind - beautiful, powerful and emotional memories which I'll never forget. It was an experience I will treasure for the rest of my life.

From the apprehension before the game - an apprehension which held us back in confirming what we just couldn't believe was about to happen - to the bewilderment of the first goal - to the wave after wave of blue and white attacks which were stopped over and over again by the Dagenham keeper.

So many memories and I'm not going to try and deliver some kind of match report for you to read. It won't do what happened any justice.

You were there. You were either there at the game or you were there in some other way - either listening to the radio or watching the match updates from wherever you were.

You were there - even if you weren't...

I remember Bodin. I remember him twisting and turning before putting the ball where it belonged. I remember going numb with joy. I remember looking around and feeling proud to be standing on the steps of the Blackthorn End with all of you as we shouted and cheered and smiled.

I remember being packed in - shoulder to shoulder with thousands of you. I remember feeling part of something truly special. I remember feeling lost and alone when Matty missed so near to the end of the game. I remember feeling vulnerable and not knowing what to do. I remember everything just seemed to become slow and yet fast at the same time. I remember not being able to think - but I knew I could still see what was happening.

I remember seeing a ball appear from behind the giant head in front of me. I remember it hit the post. And then I remember the most incredible elation I'll probably ever know. That's what I remember. I didn't see the right foot. But I saw and heard everything else.

I remember seeing Gasheads trying to escape from the Blackthorn End. They were jumping up and down so hard - it looked as if they were trying to break out of the ground through the stone steps. I remember tears and I remember faces stunned. I remember eyes dazed in disbelief. I remember heads in hands as grown men cried. I remember the sea of blue and white pouring onto the pitch at the final whistle and I remember the dancing and singing that was taking place as a giant inflatable ball was being tossed into the air. And then I remember someone saying, *"The Accrington game must be over. That's two minutes gone!"*

That's when I heard the sound I will never forget. A sound like a wave of sheer elation holding onto one hundred and thirty three years of heart and fight and tradition and pride and unity - and togetherness.

It was her sound. It rose from within the centre of the pitch and spread outwards to touch each and every one of us.

We sing her song and her words are faithful and true. And in that moment at that time - she announced herself through us. The Roar of the Rovers was Irene.

I remember the players running towards the Blackthorn End in triumph I remember Darrell being held close and kissed by supporters. I remember Wael being carried down Gloucester Road as the twilight of time embraced a beginning and an end. And as he was held aloft to the hundred-voice-cry of, *"We've got our Rovers back!"* - I truly felt as if I'd arrived at my own time in our club's time.

This time feels right for me. I'm sitting outside as I write these words and there's a grey sky of cloud which sits above a warm breeze - and it has the feel of a storm coming.

Memories of warmth and thunder growing up as a young boy in Africa. I love the way it makes me feel.

It's as if the air is charged with something as the grey sky darkens and that energy seems to touch something within me - a touch which awakens as sense of life and peace.

It's happening right now and as I feel it - I feel it hold another part of my life which I'm truly grateful for and this too gives me peace. And it's the same peace I find when I'm standing with you all on the steps of the Blackthorn End.

This sense of calmness is something I was unable to find for so long. I had to wait a long time to feel the reason for this peace because this peace is only found in belonging.

For so long I wanted to belong. I've belonged to love and loves and I've belonged to friends and others - but I've never truly felt as if I've ever belonged to a community. Until now...

There was always something missing within me and for years and years I believed the emptiness was caused by the hurt and loss I've endured in my own time. But I was wrong.

These experiences only played their part in shaping me into the man I am now. They were necessary and I'm thankful for them. It's only recently that I've realised the part that was missing was always going to be missing - until I found myself here in the West Country. I can now see how it was and remains part of the plan.

I've always felt alone and it was when I was on my own that bad things happened. But I'd always felt alone even before they happened. I spent forty five years feeling this way and then I received a welcome from the woman I now love - a welcome which was also offered by so many of you.

I now have a home and it's within our home that I know and feel I belong. And there's another place too - a place you know well. It's a place where we sing her song from heart and it's a place where we all belong.

The home of her song is where I find my peace. I don't have to look anymore. I've found a safe place where I've learned to trust again. I lost that trust in people when I was sixteen. But Irene and those who follow her have helped me to find it again. And I'm truly grateful.

From highs to lows to cries of elation to grief at losing - it's within this experience I've found my peace. The West Country gave me a new life. Bristol Rovers gave me a home.

I'm seven days away from being six years sober. On the 7th of June 2010 - I was a broken man in a homeless hostel and all I had to my name was a bag of rags for clothes. I now know that I had to be broken to be rebuilt. It just had to be that way for me. They took me away and helped me to find hope again.

If had to - I'd go through it all again to be here and to witness a right foot and the elation which followed. It was a richness within a time in a place which will forever be special to me. And it will forever be special because I shared it with you.

From Ragbag to Riches. I think I've arrived. UTG!

Memories of 7th May 2016

It was done. We made club history by winning back to back promotions - just before the twilight of day. And I still can't believe it all happened.

But it did happen. With heart and fight and history and tradition and Darrell Clarke and his squad and his managerial staff and Wael Al-Qadi and Steve Hamer and so many others - not forgetting us.

Gasheads. Faithful and True featured memories from supporters about their Twerton years. So I wanted to do something similar within these pages. So I asked supporters for their own memories of what happened only a few weeks ago.

In the end - we did it together. So here they are:

Adie White just after Brown scored the winning goal

"In my 28 years of supporting the Gas I don't think I have ever felt shock, elation and fear all at the same time as much as in this picture. Shock of seeing the ball hit the back of the net having written off our chances following Matty Taylor's uncharacteristic miss in the 88th minute. Elation of the ball falling to the wrong guy in the right place at the right time. Lee Brown our long serving, loyal left back with a sweet left foot blasting the ball home with his right foot! Time standing still as the ball seemed to take an eternity to finally cross the line, much like Igoe's injury time winner at Wembley nine years earlier. Fear of knowing that Accrington were peppering the Stevenage goal and our hearts could be cruelly broken, as they often have been following Rovers, at any second. It was very nearly too much too comprehend in one go!" **Adie White**

"Don't know. Can't remember. Still a blur!" **Neil Shortman**

"I was in my usual seat in the Drybuild stand. I have never been so tense in a match. Shot after shot. Save after save until at last, with time ticking away – we scored! Who scored? It didn't matter, we scored! The elation was incredible, hugs, kisses, high fives, brilliant. I shall never forget the shear joy on everyone's faces, what a day, what a game and what a team!" **Bob Bruton**

"Just remember tears of joy and saying YES YES FUCKING YES" **Carl Palmer**

"Mine was one of pure joy as the ball came off the post and there was Lee Brown to tap it in and I planted a kiss on Linda Hay as we jumped for joy once the Accrington result came through!" **Alan Gregory**

"My memory was at the final whistle. I cheered then looked at my mates. *"Now the wait"* I said as my mates brother tried to get a Wifi signal, the crowd cheering on the pitch then a cheer that got louder and louder. The result was in. We were going up. I hugged my mate. His brother leapt on my back. We high fived strangers. Wonderful just wonderful." **Martin Smith**

"All I can remember is screaming, *"We've done it! We've fucking gone and done it!"* while kissing and hugging some random person!" **Laura Louisee Parkin**

"Waiting nervously for the other result to come in. Then sheer madness when it did!" **Andrew Hogg**

"Mine was looking up at the sky and saying to my brother Paul Withey, *This is for you Bro!*" **Brendan Withey**

"Memories of desolation entering stoppage time! Go on Matty! Oh no! Hit the post! GOAL!!!!!!!!!!!!! Absolute pandemonium on the terraces. Never witnessed this in 50 years of supporting. Final whistle - onto the pitch with everyone. What's Accrington score? Come on – please – please! Then the almighty roar! YESSSSSSSSSSS we are going up we are going up! What scenes and memories?! Will last forever. The journey back home to North Devon has never felt so enjoyable." **Andrew Pettey**

"Pacing up and down my kitchen like an expectant father, watching Sky sports waiting for the final whistle to blow - then waiting for the Accrington final whistle. Was shaking with excitement for a couple of hours then celebrated with a cold pint of Thatchers in Romsey, Hampshire." **Jenny Bell**

"The happiness on my son's face when it sank in we'd won! Him hugging D.C as he left the Mem! Us Gas Girls dressing as pirates and the pitch invasion and Gloucester Road after party! There is no way I can pick just one moment of that day!" **Elizabeth Ann Jordan**

"For me, it was the noise. I was sat in my seat in the South Stand with my mum, my carer, we'd seen everyone run on the pitch but knew it wasn't safe for me without my wheelchair. So we waited as much for the crowds from our stand to clear as waiting for the Accy score to come in. That roar when it went up was my sign for my mum to go and get my wheelchair to push me onto the pitch. I wasn't missing out!" **Zoe Young Kirkby**

"Standing rooted to the spot in shock. Our whistle had gone. Sarah Foreman and Claire Brooks staring at each other and me - then this scream and we danced hugging each other and our Brandon Lee Gardener whooping in total ecstasy Our world stood still then erupted in pandemonium!!! **Patricia Gardener**

"The pure joy of knowing that we were nearly there...then the reality of waiting for the final whistle to go at the Accrington game. Standing in the Blackthorn End – dumbstruck. There's not a lot of things that leave me speechless but I honestly could not speak.! Looking around me and seeing other fans in the same boat. I will never, ever forget that day." **Sue Tooze**

"As normal we took up our place on the halfway line of the west enclosure, earlier than normal, so we wouldn't be struggling as was the clamor for these last and special home games of what has been a fantastic season! But with the Daggers early blow - the nerves set in! And as time ticked down with us all knowing one goal is all we need Matty Taylor strikes the post and the man of the moment Lee Brown taps in a goal of which legends are made! Que the scenes and celebrations which I can't put into words. All I can finish with is the pride in my club, manager, players, owners and of course fellow Gasheads who shared this extra special season. Gashead by birth!" **Kev Brain**

"I stood at the back of the north terrace under the walkway watching the game while an old face from Rovers I recognised from over the years stood listening back against the wall - unable to watch as time after time we all turned around in sheer frustration, berating our luck. I never did see him after the 92nd minute as our eyes were fixed on the game and mobile phones!" **Mark Revill**

"Going on the pitch knowing that they had done their job but not knowing if it would be enough and then the roar going up !! The joy, the relief the sheer ecstasy of that moment and the following few hours of celebration was something else! UTG" **Dave Camm**

"All season I believed we could do this but with ten minutes to go, after blasting shot after shot at their keeper, who seemed like he was auditioning for the next roll of superman, I did have a doubt. But knowing what Rovers are renowned for - playing to the whistle - I never gave up hope. When Matty struck the post, my heart sank - but only for a brief second as Lee Brown was there to slot this one in with his right foot too! Tears again as I write this! I couldn't breath as I was waiting for the Accrington result to come in! Rovers, you'll never know how much I love you!"

Mandy Bithell

"For me being the only gas head without a hangover Sunday Morning. I'm on tablets so couldn't drink."
Richard Skuse

"Went absolutely fucking ballistic! As soon as the whistle went I headed straight for DC to tell him we had done it! Best moment ever! I think I was erect and think I probably still am! **Ashley Belsten**

"Watching the live stream from the Blackthorn End just before midnight from Hong Kong. Seeing all the missed chances and the reaction of the fans was just like being there. Watching all the video clips within minutes after we did it was simply incredible. Didn't sleep for ages that night watching them all!!" **Glen Fry**

"Eating a pasty at the back of the Blackthorn. The tension of the game had got to me. People near me praying. People cursing our bad luck and resigned to the lottery of the playoffs! I couldn't see all of the pitch. I didn't want to look anyway. Then a HUGE roar engulfed the Mem! The roar will be remembered forever! It was our very own roar of the Rovers! The roar that shook the Mem to its core!"
John Murphy

"The whole match was spent with one eye on the pitch and one on my phone, allowing me to keep track of the live Oxford and Accrington scores. I would say it was possibly the quietest I have ever been at a game due to concentrating on three matches and the nerves running through me. The frustration at the Daggers keeper for being so damn good on the day! Watching from the Blackthorn End and behind the target as we fired one after another after another. Watching the extra time running out while still making sure Accrington hadn't scored and praying for a miracle to happen. Then it did!

Standing on the pitch sharing the euphoric atmosphere and slowly but surely letting it all sink in on what we had just accomplished. This moment can rank a solid third behind the birth of my son and my wedding. Remembering I had my celebratory cigar in my pocket that I had been saving all season and now realising the result meant that wrapper could finally be taken off. It didn't stay in my mouth for long though as a certain Matty Taylor snatched it clean out of mine and placed it in to his for a very memorable 'selfie'!! A historic moment that I am so proud to have witnessed." **Dave Turley** (Pic on next page)

Dave Turley with Matty Taylor

"I was strangely not very nervous at all. I just knew we were going to do it and true to Rovers form it was last minute! But thank God I was right! I screamed, cried and jumped around like a loony! Thanks to the guy on my right, who had tears streaming down his face, for grabbing my and planting a great big kiss on me ha ha!! What a day!"
Kim Haynes

Beth Styles with Wael Al-Qadi after Browner's right foot

"That deafening ROAR as the Accrington final score came through will live with me forever!! RTID!!!" **Helen Styles**

"Thought our chance had gone when Matty Taylor put his shot wide with 2 minutes to go. Bloke next to me was so convinced it was in, he was still celebrating whilst Daggers took the goal kick. Didn't think we'd get another chance. Then up pops Browner and the roar that greeted that goal was the loudest I can remember in 35 years of watching the Gas. Like the moment Manse's penalty hit the net last year, the ground shook. I then tried to keep my camera steady in amongst all the mayhem. (Pic below) **Rick Weston**

"That moment the whistle went and we were relegated two years ago, a wave of silence fell over the mem. It was one of the strangest feelings you could imagine. It felt like for a minute we were all in this limbo, coming to terms with the realism of what had just happened. Then on Saturday, the complete opposite! A wave of euphoria that swept the Mem when the Accrington result came through. It seemed to start at the far end of the East stand, and when it hit you, it instantly made you feel incredible. All the pain of relegation suddenly felt worth it." **Sam Bishop**

"Before the game Stu Sinclair arranged to meet my eight year old Ben for his birthday. Ben has a rare condition called Sturge Weber which causes seizures and learning difficulties. So Stu kindly agreed to give him a signed photo and offered to meet him. He gave Ben three photos and a card signed by the squad and it was the best start to a match possible! Thank you Stu for being the star you are.

Anyway this season, every time I have taken my child to the toilet or gone for a cigarette - Rovers seemed to score. So smuch so that the guys who sit next to me would tell me to piss off when the ball wouldn't go in.

So when Daggers scored - off I went! I spent pretty much the next 80 minutes of the game trying to smoke my tension away and hoping my lucky streak would carry us to victory. Watched most of it from behind the bars of the south stand smoking area. Saw Bodin's goal from that spot and had my daughter come looking for me at half time as she thought I may have had a heart attack (love the fact she didn't check till half time, so caring).

I gave up on the 89 minute and went back to my seat only to see Taylor miss, shortly followed by Browner's goal. What a rush! Never felt anything like it, looked around to see my daughter and elder son screaming and going mental with my six year old crying with shock from the noise. Best day of my family's life. The joy, pleasure and excitement of what makes Rovers so special in a way no other team could. **Wayne Prewett**

"I didn't know who the goal scorer was as I had my hands on my head after Taylor's shot hit the post - but then a second later I see the ball being tapped in for a rebound! Even the reporters for Final Score and Soccer Saturday initially didn't know who scored the winner but when the ball went in it was mayhem and pure elation and delirium from everyone!" **Aidaroes Mohamed**

"So many memories, but standing at the Vic looking up Gloucester Road and seeing the players being carried on fans shoulders brought a rush of pure happiness. When a little later I looked up and saw Wael being carried high I was just stood in amazement and sang louder than I had all day!" **Timothy Ford**

"Watching the drama unfold on Soccer Saturday with my three year old, wishing I could be there with the rest of my family, watching chance after chance go begging, turning the live stream on and then off repeatedly not coping with watching it live. Waiting for Jeff to just say we'd scored, thinking it just wasn't going to be our day, then the joy, the relief when the goal went in The agonising wait as we waited for the final whistle at Accrington. Jumping around the house when we knew we'd done it!" **Kim Price** "My overriding memory is falling to the floor after Taylor missed, feeling that was it we had blown it. When Browner scored the roar was the best I have heard supporting Rovers. For me pure relief we had done our bit and won regardless of other results. Being on the pitch felt surreal. I found a Rovers mate who's Dad had just died and said to him he's looking down at you right now celebrating. It was pure celebration - last year was relief and redemption. I have never felt so many emotions as I did Saturday. Being a Gashead at this time could not have felt any better. Pure elation! UTG" **Jamie Stockley**

"The whole day was just amazing. Started by putting my new Gas number plate on the car and then early into the pub. The relief when Bodin went on his mazy run and equalised. Tearing the last of my hair out as all those chances went begging. Browners goal was unreal, couldn't believe it. Then on the pitch as soon as the whistle went, didn't wait for Accrington score. I knew we were up. Then on the pitch when Jamie Stockley said, "Your dads watching!" just made the day for me. Left me speechless. Magic!" **Richard Wood**

"The whole day was amazing. Massive queues before they opened the gates, the importance of equalising quickly, the total effort and 'never say die' attitude bringing wave after wave of attack. When Taylor shot wide in the 90th minute - we still kept pressing. But the best moment was the low of Taylor hitting the post - but the elation when Browner guided home the rebound! The ecstasy and relief poured out and there was bedlam all around the ground and will never be forgotten. Wow what a day! UTG" **Dale Jacobs** (Pic below)

"My eldest son Matthew and me on the terrace and the pitch with our ginger Gaffney wigs high-fiving. The relief of that goal by Brown and the joy of everyone around. We managed to get in a fair few pictures and on TV with our wigs which means the day is captured for prosperity. He's only in his second full season and he's already seen two promotions. Could be worse! UTG!" **Andrew Brace**

"Standing in the Blackthorn in the first minute of injury time and Roman asking Tara if I was alright as my right leg was twitching uncontrollably. I wasn't that nervous at Wembley when we went to penalties. My youngest, Kieran with his hands over his eyes and Luke shaking his head as Matty Taylor hit the post! Then, pandemonium and my leg stopped twitching and I knew we were going up. Then the whistle went and everyone was on the pitch and Tara and me said to the boys, not until it's official. Then that spine tingling roar when the result came through and we went onto the pitch with thousands of our brothers and sisters to celebrate. And I will say it took all my will power not to cry at the relief and the sheer pleasure at being there!" **Don Wilson**

"For me, it was looking skyward after about twenty minutes and seeing them. They were here and I knew in my heart that we would go up. As there were more than usual. I really knew we would be promoted. I didn't know how or the score, but I knew. I turned to my friend Patricia Gardener and with a big grin on my face said, *"It's ok Pat, we're going up, don't worry."* I pointed to the sky, *"My lucky seagulls are here!"* **Dawn Talbot**

"Watching remotely from Sussex. Exiled at the age of 9 now 52 but still Gas. A wife and son who simply don't get it. Sitting, phone in hand, update after update from whatever source I could find. 1-0 down, 1-1 (of course) no nerves, 80 mins, 90 mins, so many missed chances. But I knew it and then 92 mins - Goal. Simply smiled. My Rovers, my club, my team. The hard way, as it's always been. Live on. Never die. Never give up. BRFC." **Steven Betteridge**

"Sharing the experience with my 11yr old son. Dancing with him on the pitch. I told him to take a mental picture of the celebrations and lock them away in his head. Learn from the team that with determination and hard work you can make your dreams come true!" **Joanne McGarry**

"Been a Gashead all my life. Had a season ticket from age two. Not missed a game all season so to go up was special - but the atmosphere was electric. I've never seen the whole ground on their feet singing - but the chorus of goodnight Irene between the goal and full time involved everyone! And the scenes on Gloucester Road were incredible." **William Powell**

"The feeling from the roar when the final score for the Accrington match came through (gives me goosebumps now just thinking of it) and then grabbing my sons hand and running as fast as my little legs could onto the pitch and seeing my 12 year old that happy was an amazing feeling!! And Don, Roman literally thought you were gonna have a meltdown!" **Tara James**

"My son, who was at the Mem, beamed back the last 10 minutes to me here in New Zealand via Skype and it was without doubt the most dramatic ten minutes in my 45 years of supporting the Rovers. It was 4:00am here and I was screaming the place down. Goodness only knows what the neighbours thought!" **Jeff Short**

"For me, it was the sheer volume of the roar that erupted on the terraces when Lee Brown fired the ball and us into League One. My heart pounding, everyone cheering, thousands of Gasheads jumping up and down in jubilation, yet everything seemed to stand still and silent for a few seconds. It's all a blur – what just happened. Then I realised it wasn't a dream and I thought to myself, "We are Bristol Rovers. Now we know!" **Joey Drewett**

"Standing in the Blackthorn with my 13 year old grandson (4th generation Gashead) and two sons. Seeing Daggers score early on and thinking - why do we never do this the easy way?! Then protecting my grandson from the surge following Bodin's brilliant goal. Matty's miss on 88 minutes and going into added time and me thinking bugger. Play-offs again. Step up Matty's great shot followed by Lee Brown's right-footed score. I tried to shield my grandson again but I was swept away down the terrace in a flood of jubilant Gasheads. I kept my feet until I crashed against the perimeter fence. I had an idea that I saw. It was 2-1!! The noise was indescribable. I clambered back up the terrace to pacify my grandson who thought I had been trampled. Final whistle. Full throated Goodnight Irene from all round the ground. And two minutes later another huge roar greeted the Accrington score. I have never invaded the pitch before in 60 years supporting, but hey - it had to be done. The four of us embracing on the pitch. Never to be forgotten!" **Stephen Foulkes**

"Myself and stepson have been going when we can to games home and away with my plan to convince him that Bristol Rovers is the team to support - rather than watch the so-called 'superstars' of the Premiership. I was flying back from Spain that morning and was in two minds about going as I had that feeling that we were going to be bridesmaids again. But he convinced me we had to go. It was also the first game since he was 18 so we could soak up the atmosphere after he bought me my first pint! When the second goal went in I knew my job was done, another Gashead for life who got what it's all about!" **James Hibbs**

"OMG! Where do I start? A few months ago hubby had his shifts changed at work which enabled him to see all of the last 4 home games. Browner scoring & the roar when the Accrington game finished. There are no words to describe it. We just looked at each other & cried & going down Gloucester Road and seeing the raod closed due to all the Gasheads and players having shoulder rides!"

Janet Davis

"Standing in the East Terrace Enclosure getting soaked from the downpour when the heavens opened using a flag to shield us. I watched the game with my son Zac, aged six, and it was his first game and lifting him over the barrier when the final whistle and joining in with the celebrations on the pitch with everyone! Then it was time to join in with the celebrations down Gloucester Road for the night and then waking up with a hangover from hell on the Sunday morning. UTG" **Craig Stooke**

"Watched the game with my dad (in his 70s) and my 5 year old. My son wondered why I had tears in my eyes when Browner scored? I had to tell him that the 2 promotions were not normal and that was only the 4th one I'd witnessed in thirty five years. Happy days. He then had to tell his class in Truro all about his weekend and the mighty Gas!" **Martin Lewis**

"Having watched Rovers from Tote to Trumpton - I fell away from going to all matches for a while until they hit the Vanarama. There was something about that season that reeled me back in and I started to love going again. Nights against Brentry and Gateshead seemed special again. Maybe it's that Dunkirk spirit thing!!. Since then I have not missed a home game and have loved it all. However, I stupidly missed out on organising myself a ticket for the Daggers game so was confined to listening from home near the old Gasworks. On the final whistle I went berserk and jumped on my bike and rode up to the Mem. I was screaming my head off riding through St Werbs and it was up through Ashley Down that I was captured on camera by some bloke in his car.

It's funny how a good picture can encapsulate a moment better than anything. I am truly grateful to the person who snapped me. Maybe more people will now join me cycling to watch the Rovers. Am thinking about going to an away game next season on my bike. Anyway what a day with the love of my life. Gashead on a Bike !!!! **Daniel Hill**

DANIEL HILL

ABOUT THE AUTHOR

John Thomson is an author, documentary filmmaker and Gashead living in Bristol. He lives with his partner Helen and her two daughters – Beth and Meg

Printed in Great Britain
by Amazon